COACHING AND TEACHING GENERATION Z

"HONOR THE RELATIONSHIPS"

BRIAN POLIAN

ISBN: 978-1-60679-597-2
Book layout: Cheery Sugabo
Cover design: Cheery Sugabo
Front cover photos: Courtesy of Gus Stark and LSU Athletics / Courtesy of Katie Meyers and Notre Dame Athletics
Back cover photo: Courtesy of Joe Ginley and JCU Athletics

Coaches Choice
P.O. Box 1828
Monterey, CA 93942
www.coacheschoice.com

DEDICATION

For my wife, Laura, and my children, Aidan and Charlotte. I am so grateful for our family and the joy that you all bring to my life.

I Love You—Always and Forever

ACKNOWLEDGMENTS

The idea for this book was born in December of 2019, after listening to two great teachers talk about how important relationships were in effectively connecting with and teaching young men. For weeks, I could not get the idea out of my head. It was a very simple concept, but one that I felt is taken for granted by coaches and teachers working with Generation Z.

As I decided to explore the value of relationships further, I reflected back on all of my own experiences with family, friends, teachers, and coaches. I realized how truly blessed I have been to have so many people who have loved, supported, and influenced me throughout my life, my career, and this project. Without all of those people, my own journey, while incomplete, would not have been possible.

William Arthur Ward once said, "Feeling gratitude and not expressing it is like wrapping a present and not giving it." I want to make sure that I take this opportunity to express the immense gratitude I have for those important people in my life.

I don't know if I am lucky or simple, but I found my calling at 14-years old. In the summer of 1989, I worked as a ball boy at training camp for the Buffalo Bills. I watched the head coach, Marv Levy, attack each day with energy and joy. I was fascinated with the way he interacted with the team and how he approached each player individually. I thought to myself, "That is what I want to do with my life." I knew then I was going to be a coach. Marv Levy has been an important mentor from the very beginning of my career and I am so grateful for the impact he has had on my life. Other coaches on those Buffalo Bills teams influenced me as well. I appreciate Elijah Pitts, Don Lawrence, Bruce DeHaven, Ted Marchibroda, and Walt Corey for allowing me to hang around, pester them with questions, and learn from them.

If we are lucky, we find people in our lives that leave a lasting impression and help guide us as we grow. I was fortunate to have a handful of people like that in my own life. Leonard Coppola was the best youth-sports coach I have ever had and influences my style of teaching to this day. Jerry Smith, John Scibetta, and Tony Giardina all looked out for me during my high school years at St. Francis. John Storey was my position coach in college at John Carroll University and showed me how important it was for a coach to love his players. Finally, my "Intro to the Civil War" professor, Chris Phillips. He is the single best teacher I have ever encountered in a classroom, and he ignited my passion for history.

I have worked for and with some incredible people in this profession. Looking back, I learned a something from each one of them. I can only hope to have the impact on young people that these men have had on the players they've coached. Jim Hofher gave me my first full-time job in college football at the University at Buffalo and is one of the finest men I know.

Head coaches like Brian Kelly, David Shaw, Kevin Sumlin, David Cutcliffe, Derek Mason, and Pat Fitzgerald have been important and generous role models. Veteran assistants like Bill Lewis, John Latina, Dave Huxtable, Ron Lynn, Jim Bollman, Gary Tranquill, and Randy Hart were so kind in helping me develop in my early years. There are peers that have been incredibly influential as well, and I am so grateful for them. Lester Erb, Clark Lea, Mike Bradeson, Terry Joseph, Amy Bokker, Matt House, Brick Haley, and many others; all of these coaches served as examples of how to do it the right way.

For this book, specifically, there were current and former players who shared their time and insights. It would have been impossible to complete this without them. Ryan Harris, Jody Owens, Asauni Rufus, James Butler, Don Jackson, Ahki Muhammad, Ricky Thomas Jr, Daelin Hayes, and Shaun Crawford were all thoughtful and honest with their perspectives. I am truly grateful for their willingness to participate.

There were also coaches from across the country who were kind enough to contribute to this project. They came from different sports and different levels of competition, but all had one thing in common, my respect and admiration for each. Thank you to Chuck Kyle, Marv Levy, Scott Fitch, Paul Mainieri, Jill Phillips, Jerry Smith, Pat Fitzgerald, Cheston Blackshear, Brick Haley, Deanna Gumpf, Sean Sweeney, and John Rittman.

I had a couple of valuable advocates during the early stages of the manuscript and I appreciate their time and patience. My sister-in-law, Amanda Maggiotto, is one of the smartest and toughest women I know, and her feedback was very helpful. Nick Lezynski, Steve Hunter, and Tina Segan Hunter served as proofreaders and were generous with their time as well. Fr. Nate Wills, Fr. Paul Doyle, and Dr. Bob Laurent were kind enough to be available to talk through some of the concepts with me. Brian Kelly, Jack Swarbrick, and Rob Kelly from Notre Dame all encouraged this undertaking, and I appreciated their support a great deal. Stephanie Rempe and Michael Bonnette from LSU and Joe Ginley from John Carroll University were incredibly helpful as we took on a 2nd edition, and I am grateful for their help as well.

I have a wonderful family, starting with incredible parents. My father, Bill, is the most influential person in my life, both personally and professionally. My mother, Eileen, is the foundation of the family and models love and loyalty every day of her life. These two special people are the ones that first showed me the importance of loving relationships. My sister, Lynn, and my brothers, Chris and Dennis, are all accomplished professionals. More importantly, they are honest, sincere, and caring human beings. I am grateful for them, their spouses, and all my nieces and nephews.

Finally, I want to thank my wife, Laura, and my children, Aidan and Charlotte. Becoming a parent was the greatest joy of my life and it affected me deeply as a coach. When I would tell a recruit's family, "I will care for your child as if he were my own,"

I never understood the gravity of that statement. Welcoming Aidan and Charlotte into our lives helped me better appreciate the amount of trust parents are placing with coaches. They also taught me patience, understanding, and unconditional love. Laura is my partner, and there is no one else with whom I would rather be on this journey. She is strong, smart, principled, loyal, and loving. She helped guide me through this book, as she has helped guide me through the last 23 years of our lives together. My life has been filled with so many blessings, but none more so than finding Laura.

FOREWORD

The relationships between a coach and his players are essential to winning in any form—on the field, in the classroom, and in life. Players need to trust their coaches and be willing to listen and learn in a positive coaching environment. In order to develop that trust, the coaches need to work purposefully at building those relationships. At Notre Dame and at LSU, we emphasize the strengthening of the connection between coach and player. It is as important as any technical or tactical teaching that we do. As a result, we have a positive and consistent culture within our program. It also one of the reasons that we have enjoyed success on the field.

I believe that the building of relationships is important in recruiting as well. It is vital that we invest the time to build a rapport and get to know our recruits and their families. It lays a foundation of understanding and fosters growth when they arrive on our campus. I know, for certain, that the open and honest communication that we kept with our prospects and their parents is one of the reasons we consistently recruited top 10 classes at Notre Dame, and will continue to do so now at LSU.

When I brought Brian Polian back to Notre Dame as our special teams coordinator/ recruiting coordinator in 2017, and then onto to LSU in 2021, I knew I was getting a hard-charging coach who loved the game of football. I also saw a coach who was re-dedicating himself to being better connected with the players. Brian was working day to day to build close relationships with members of our own team, prospects, and their families. Through open communication and honest conversations, he built trust around our special teams units and our recruiting program. Players on our teams and high school athletes abroad bought in and we have seen the payoff. They all recognize that he is invested not only in their success as football players at one of the top programs in the country, but that he has a desire to set them up for success for the rest of their lives. I am excited to see him incorporate that same approach as he leads the athletics department at his alma mater, John Carroll University. The university and all of its student-athletes will be better off for it!

—Brian Kelly
Head Football Coach
Louisiana State University

CONTENTS

Dedication . . . 3
Acknowledgments . . . 4
Foreword . . . 7
Introduction . . . 10

Chapter 1: Relationships Are the Reward . . . 13
Chapter 2: Why Relationships Are Important . . . 21
Chapter 3: The Building Blocks of Relationships . . . 29
Chapter 4: How to Build Better Relationships . . . 41
Chapter 5: Consumer Relationships vs. Covenant Relationships . . . 49
Chapter 6: The Dynamics of Diversity and Inclusion on Relationships . . . 57
Chapter 7: Who Is Generation Z? . . . 71
Chapter 8: Connecting With Generation Z . . . 77
Chapter 9: Giving Generation Z Feedback . . . 83
Chapter 10: Generation Z and Adversity . . . 93
Chapter 11: Valued Perspectives . . . 103

About the Author . . . 119

INTRODUCTION

In December of 2019, I was sitting with Brian Kelly, then the head football coach at Notre Dame, in the office of Alex Zaqueira, the headmaster of St. John's High School in Shrewsbury, MA. We were in town for a recruiting visit and had a couple of moments to visit, before we were to meet with the prospect. Coach Kelly and Alex were swapping stories about growing up in Massachusetts and the rivalries amongst the private school hockey programs in the state. St. John's is an all-boys school, so the topic shifted to working with and teaching young men. Coach Kelly asked Mr. Zaqueira, after all his years at the school, what was the single most important thing he's learned about trying to connect with high school-age boys. Alex did not miss a beat and replied:

"We have to *honor the relationship*, before we can honor the task."

When I walked away from that conversation between two teachers of men, I was energized. My mind was racing with thoughts about this generation of young people with whom we work every single day. I considered how different their world is from the one I grew up in, the challenges they face, and how they demand more from their teachers and coaches. I made a decision to re-dedicate myself to being better at building relationships with student-athletes. I wanted to find ways to better connect. Not only to help improve their performance on the field, but also in hopes of becoming a more positive influence in their lives.

The first thing that we have to remind ourselves in coaching is that *all human beings have an inherent desire to be close to other people.* We are all social creatures. By relating to other people, we feel worthy and are provided a sense of belonging. There is term used in football to describe a certain type of player. He's called a "relationship guy." It essentially means that you will not see this player's best until he feels comfortable with and trusts the people he's working with. In reality, all people are "relationship guys" to a certain degree! As coach or a teacher, to ignore this is to ignore human nature. That is why building healthy relationships with our players is the first and most important step in our journey with them.

Like anything else in life, if you want to be good at building relationships, it takes work. Finding ways to connect, to build bridges, is a skill. As a skill, it can be improved and finely tuned with repetition. Interacting with the players and paying attention to the relationships that we are building has to be a priority and something that we think about every day.

I set out on a journey to learn more about Generation Z and why relationships are so important in connecting with them. I also wanted to explore the building blocks of relationships and ways to improve them. Along the way, I reflected back on all the experiences I had throughout the course of my own career. I recognized the areas I did well and also areas I needed to improve. More than anything, I was reminded what makes our profession so special—the relationships with the players. Those relationships are the reward for coaches and the staff.

This book began as an outline of my thoughts on the relationships we have with our athletes. I simply wanted to write them down in order to keep them organized. It then morphed into a lecture I gave at a coaching clinic. It was literally a PowerPoint presentation. The talk was well received, and a couple of high school coaches commented that it was a topic that deserved more attention. While I appreciated the feedback, I didn't think it was possible to grow it any further, given the time constraints of life as a college football coach.

In mid-March of 2020, our global community suffered a pandemic with the outbreak of the Covid-19 virus. Like everyone else in the country, our lives at Notre Dame came to a screeching halt. In the weeks to come, I began to feel anxious and restless. After 23 years of consistency, my life was thrown out of whack, and I was finding it difficult to find daily purpose. I expressed those feelings to my wife, Laura, and to my father, Bill.

Separate of one another, each challenged me to make use of the time the quarantine provided and to take on a project that I would not normally have the opportunity to tackle. I decided I wanted to write about relationships between coaches and players, specifically in regards to Generation Z. I wanted to provide perspective, awareness, and some tools to help other coaches and teachers improve in this area.

In December of 2020, the first edition of this work was published. As it began to gain traction, I was very surprised by some of the feedback. When I first began the project, I thought that I was writing this "little book" that might be of service to coaches and maybe, some teachers. What I learned quickly was that there are many different people, in various walks of life, who work closely with Generation Z, and they were gaining some insight from it. In June 2021, my agents, Trace Armstrong and Kyle McCarthy, were generous and trusting enough to allow me to present on working with Generation Z at an event geared for executives, professionals, and coaches from various backgrounds across business and sports. That opportunity opened new doors, introduced me to new people, and started conversations that helped me learn more about Gen Z and what makes them so unique. I went all the way from talking to head coaches in the NFL to sharing ideas with faculty at an Ivy League institution. It was surreal.

In late November of 2021, life really got turned upside down. Brian Kelly, in a surprise to many, decided to leave Notre Dame and take on the challenge of rebuilding an LSU football program that had gone from a National Champion to a sub-500 team in a little over two years. Coach Kelly asked me to join him in Louisiana, and I was excited about the opportunity. I arrived in Baton Rouge in early December, and my family joined me the following March. All the things that I wrote about in terms of building new relationships and connecting with young people were being put to the test at a new program, in a different part of the country. It was both exhilarating and nerve-wracking at the same time.

Following the 2022 season, I did some serious reflection on where I was in my career. Most importantly, I examined where I was in regard to being a father and a husband. In my heart, I knew it was time to shift my focus and to be more present for my family, and specifically for my children, as they enter a critical time in their lives and development. In the spring of 2023, I made the decision to return to my alma mater, John Carroll University, a Jesuit institution in Northeast Ohio with a rich athletic tradition. In my new role as Director of Athletics I hope to utilize the lessons I have learned in coaching across 24 varsity sports and improve the experience of more than 700 student-athletes. In the second edition of *Coaching and Teaching Generation Z*, I have added some thoughts and cleaned up some others as these new experiences have helped sharpen my view even further. I hope it helps.

—Brian Polian
June 2023

CHAPTER 1

Relationships Are the Reward

In the summer of 2016, I was entering my fourth season as the head coach at the University of Nevada and was excited about our team and the season to come. On June 10 of that year, we lost a beloved teammate and friend, when Marc Ma drowned in an accident in Lake Tahoe, only 30 minutes from our campus in Reno. Unfortunately, another teammate and a handful of other student-athletes from other sports had witnessed the accident. I was in Chicago at the time, participating in a football camp at Northwestern University with two of our assistant coaches, Lester Erb and Cheston Blackshear. We were on the field when we got the call.

Lucas Weber, one of our players and a close friend of Marc's, called me to alert me that there had been accident. He then passed the phone to a member of local law enforcement who told me there was a search and rescue going on, but that I needed to be prepared for it to turn into a "search and recovery." I was stunned. The air came out of me. My good friend, Pat Fitzgerald, head coach at Northwestern, allowed me to use his office, as I tried to gather myself, alert our administration to the situation, and get myself back to Reno.

Making the call to Marc's parents that evening was the most difficult thing I have ever had to do. The next day, back in Reno, we brought our players in quickly and directed them into the team meeting room. I had to tell them that they had lost their brother, a member of their football family, and we had to begin the healing process. Our staff and our administration would begin by offering any support we could, to both the team and Marc's family.

The 2016 season was the most tumultuous year of my coaching career. The loss of Marc transformed our summer from a time to bond as a team and develop physically, to a daily struggle of trying to hold our guys together and support them through an incredible tragedy. When football finally arrived, the adversity continued. We lost an unprecedented number of players to injuries during the season across all position groups. The most significant injuries occurred at two of our most important positions. Charlie Faraimo, our best defensive tackle, and Tyler Stewart, our starting quarterback, were both lost for the season.

We lost a couple of close games in the middle of the schedule by single-digits and criticism began to mount, but our group persevered. They loved one another and battled their tails off. At the end of the season on Senior Day, we beat Utah State on the last play of the game. Then, came the trip down south to play our rival, the UNLV Rebels, in the battle for the Fremont Cannon. We were an eight-point underdog going into the most important game on the schedule. We played beautifully that day, and I was overcome with emotion following the game. I was so proud of and happy for our team. They had been through so much and this was one of the few times that season that I saw them genuinely happy. There was a total release of relief and joy following that victory.

The following morning I was summoned to the office of the athletic director. Change was coming. He and the University president informed me that they were going in another direction and that I was being released. They allowed me to visit briefly with our staff and then have the opportunity to visit with the team, in the same spot where, six months earlier, I had to inform them of the loss of their friend.

It was incredibly difficult to stand up in front of the team to tell them that I was no longer going to be their coach. My emotions were raw and hard to manage. It was a combination of exhaustion at the end of a difficult year, frustration over the decision that had been made, and sadness over the changes that were coming. I struggled to hold back tears, as I thanked them for everything they had given the program. I also wanted to let them know how much I appreciated them for what they had done for my family and me. Lastly, I wanted to apologize for not doing better for them. I'm sorry that I couldn't have done better.

With that, I turned and tried leave the room. Before I could, a senior-player jumped out of his seat, came over, and hugged me. He thanked me. We both began to tear up. A line had formed at the front of the room, and I was able to touch every guy, with either a handshake or an embrace. I'm not naïve; not every player was upset that a change was being made. But, I was grateful for the chance to say thanks. In the end, I had the opportunity to share a personal moment with each player. I was overcome, and I was spent. On the ride home back to my house, I drove quietly, trying to process all that had happened that morning. Not succeeding was frustrating, and saying goodbye to the young men who gave and taught me so much was terribly sad.

When I entered the profession of coaching nearly 20 years earlier, I was searching for many things. I loved the teaching part of the job and really enjoyed working with young people. But, I was also ambitious. I wanted to rise in the ranks as fast possible. I wanted to be viewed as one of the hot, young coaches in the business.

Every off-season, advancement and the congruent finances became a factor. I was trying to move out of mid-major college football. I was enamored of the Power 5 Conferences, with the huge crowds and big budgets. Even as I climbed each step of the ladder, I was focused on the next. That's not to say I wasn't trying to do a good job, I was. I loved coaching football, and I loved competing. But I would be lying if I said that professional advancement wasn't part of the equation.

The only step left on my climb was to become a head coach. In January of 2013, I achieved that dream, when I was hired at the University of Nevada, Reno. It wasn't until that journey came to a close four year later, that I truly understood I had been focused on the wrong things. My time at Nevada reminded me that the best and most rewarding part of the job is the *relationships.* That's all I could think about on that ride home from the office—how lucky I was to be a part of the lives of all of those players and coaches.

I would imagine that some sports fans would hear that statement and think to themselves, "Ok, whatever." Outsiders probably assume that the chance to experience the stadiums, the crowds, and the traditions are the best part. They are cool. Tiger Stadium, or Death Valley as it is known at LSU, on a Saturday night is the stuff of legend. Walking out of the tunnel at Notre Dame Stadium on game day gave me goose bumps. Coaching and winning against Alabama at Bryant-Denny Stadium with Texas A&M is something that I will remember for the rest of my life. But it's not the best part.

Some people could look at how particular coaches are treated like pseudo-royalty on campus and in the community and think, "That must be pretty nice." Others would probably point to the way salaries have exploded in the last couple of decades and expect that money would be the most attractive part of being a coach. Those things, and a myriad of others, make being a coach in major college football a great job. But it's the *relationships* that make it a *calling.*

When my time is up, and I am no longer able to be involved in this wonderful game, it will be the relationships that I miss most. It is the things that people never see, the shared experiences that don't ever find the light of day, that make it such a wonderful profession.

A Fraternity of Brothers

John Latina, a veteran offensive-line coach who has worked at places such as Temple, Kansas State, Ole Miss, Notre Dame, and Duke, used to say that there was nothing better than a little "fellowship" amongst the staff. "Lats" and I worked together at Notre Dame, and I loved hearing him talk about working at Kansas State with Bill Snyder or at Ole Miss for David Cutcliffe. There were endless laughs, as he regaled us with stories from the practice fields and the recruiting trail.

But there were also lessons to be learned and veteran coaches can teach a young guy a lot. An aspiring coach can gain a lot of knowledge by just sitting in a hotel lobby with the older guys and simply listening. On occasion, there are some four-letter words, a great deal of laughing, and in some cases, some commiserating about our lot in life. But, there is also a lot of wisdom. Stories about being hired and being fired, about moving all over the country, about starting families, raising kids, about handling a divorce—we hear all of it. And we share all of it—like a small fraternity of brothers.

When I think about how special the relationships are on a coaching staff, one night in particular comes to mind. I was on Kevin Sumlin's first staff at Texas A&M in 2012, as the special teams coordinator/tight ends coach. That season was the first for the Aggies in the SEC. We upset #1 Alabama on the road, and Johnny Manziel won the

Heisman Trophy. It was a magical year. During training camp that August, our offensive coordinator, Kliff Kingsbury, made a deal with the offensive coaches. If we won 10 games or more, the offensive staff would have a party at the end of the year, and Kliff would pick up the tab. We beat Missouri at home in late-November to finish the season at 10-2, and Coach Kingsbury proved to be a man of his word.

In early December, the staff gathered at the home of BJ Anderson, the offensive line coach. Anyone who helped on the offensive side of the ball was invited. It was the coaches, the GA's, the analysts, and even the administrative assistants. Spouses and significant others were included as well. The best Mexican restaurant in town catered; the bar was stocked and manned with a bartender. Kliff hired Max Stalling, a Texas singer/songwriter to perform. We all sat on the deck, with a fire going and under a cloudless, star-filled Texas sky, and enjoyed the music and one another. It was one the best nights I ever had in coaching, and it was far, far away from the field.

It's not just the relationships with the other coaches either. Our football family almost always includes the people on the support staff. The trainers, the equipment people, the strength coaches, the video team, football operations—all these different folks are with us every single day and form our own little world. And with them too, we share the inside jokes and hidden struggles. Some of the most impactful moments don't take place on a field or in front of a camera. They take place at a corner table in a dining hall during the dog days of August. They take place on a charter flight from a small college airport on a Friday afternoon. They take place on a bus, idling outside a stadium, two hours after the game has finished on a Saturday night. I have learned to recognize these moments, and even more, to savor them. They are fleeting, but they are part of what make the job so incredibly cool.

People Make the Difference

With all that said, nothing compares to the bonds that we build through the relationships with our players. When anyone ever asks me what is the best part of being a coach, the answer is simple—it is the players.

We often enter the lives of these young men when they are 16 or 17 years old, when the recruiting process begins in earnest. If we are on the winning side of the recruiting battles, and they chose our schools, these families entrust us with their sons. We take on the responsibility of impacting their lives, as they go from being young adults and grow into being men. We watch them grow and develop, and if we are lucky, we are part of that development. We are welcomed into their homes and into their families.

For four or five years, we try to nurture, to demand, and to develop. We counsel them through off-field drama, we needle them about classes, we bring them to the house for dinner, we jump their butts on the practice field—all in the hopes that we can help make them better. We try to leave a positive mark on a young man during one of the most impressionable times in his life.

There are a number of relationships that I have developed through recruiting that have lasted the test of time and grown into friendships, but there is one person who comes to mind, when I think how about how meaningful these relationships can become. In my first season at Notre Dame under Charlie Weis, we recruited a safety from Youngstown, Ohio by the name of Kyle McCarthy. I had grown incredibly fond of Kyle and his family throughout the recruiting process and was pushing hard for us to offer him a scholarship. Kyle had Notre Dame roots; his older brother was attending school there at the time, and his grandfather had lettered in baseball for the Irish. We hosted Kyle and his parents for an official visit in January of 2005. My wife, Laura, and I were sitting with Kyle and his parents at dinner on a Saturday night.

Coach Weis was not able to be there that evening, because he was still coaching with the New England Patriots, who were in the NFL playoffs. He had spoken to Kyle a couple days earlier on the phone and informed him that we had decided to offer him a scholarship and that we wanted Kyle with us. I was really excited and hopeful that we could close the deal. As we wrapped up our meal, Kyle asked if we could talk. He informed us, right at the table, that he was committing and coming to Notre Dame. His father beamed and his mom began to cry, which caused my wife to cry. It was a really great moment and one that I will never forget.

Kyle went on to become a terrific special teams player, when he was young, a two-year starter as he grew older, and a captain at Notre Dame. He played a little while in

Courtesy of Katie Meyers and Notre Dame Athletics

The best coaches understand that we have to focus not only on building relationships with players, but relationships that reach out and are beneficial to them.

the NFL and later entered coaching, even spending time on the staff at his alma mater. Kyle also survived cancer, married a wonderful woman, and started a family. He is one the best people with whom I have ever had the privilege to work, remains a trusted friend, and even serves as my business advisor. A relationship like that is very special.

Working with a young person on a daily basis and watching that person grow and develop is incredible. There is nothing like celebrating a victory with a player, whether it is big or small. It brings a sense of pride—the pride you feel for the athlete and the pride you feel knowing you were a small part of it. There is also nothing like the disappointment that you feel for a player when they don't do well. You can understand their pain and you hurt, because you couldn't do more to help them.

Few things are as rewarding as hearing one of your former players express to you that you were impactful in his life. It took some time to really understand this. Mike Anello, a former walk-on at Notre Dame who went on to become one of the best special teams players in the country, once approached my father, outside the tunnel after a game. He told my dad that the opportunity and encouragement I had given him had changed his life. In reality, Mike did all the work and created his own opportunity through perseverance, but his words were incredibly kind none-the-less.

My father, Bill Polian, spent his entire adult life in football. He has been a scout, a coach, and executive for over 50 years and is enshrined in the Pro Football Hall of Fame. He understood and appreciated the gravity of what Mike had just shared with him. When my dad told me of the exchange, I was glad to hear those kind words, but I didn't quite get it. My dad took a moment to make sure I understood. He told me that I would never receive a paycheck, a championship ring, or a bowl watch that would be as meaningful as a player telling me that I had been impactful on his life. It's the players—it's the relationships with them that are the most rewarding.

Times have changed and are continuing to change. The students of today, Generation Z, are demanding more of their teachers, and the players are demanding more of their coaches. The focus is shifting to the mental, physical, and emotional well-being of the young people. Rightfully so. Gone are the days of telling a player, "Do that because I told you so." Gone are the days of casting aside any player who wouldn't do our bidding, just because we exerted power over him. Gone are the days of players achieving to the highest levels, but doing so despite their coaching.

The best coaches are adjusting to this new world. They understand that we have to focus not only on building relationships with players, but relationships that reach out and are beneficial to them. We have to build relationships that are "other-centered" and based in service. What we are learning is, that if we want players to listen so we can help them achieve to their highest potential, we have to build the solid foundation of a relationship first.

Following my dismissal at Nevada, I spent a couple of quiet weeks, reflecting on my experiences. I thought long and hard about what I did well, and more importantly, what

I did poorly and needed to fix moving forward. In January of 2017, Brian Kelly called and offered me an opportunity to return to the University of Notre Dame, a place that my wife and I loved. Our previous five years there under Charlie Weis represented the longest stay in one place during my career. We started our family there, welcoming our son, Aidan, and had him christened in the Log Chapel on campus. We developed really strong and important friendships with people in the community. It was a blessing to have the opportunity to come back.

Working for Brian Kelly is very rewarding for me personally. He has taught me a great deal. "BK" is a wonderful communicator, a natural leader, trusts his people to do their jobs, and treats the staff and their families with respect. He has also helped me to re-emphasize the importance of building relationships as a coach.

When we returned to Notre Dame in 2017, the Irish were coming off an uncharacteristic 4-8 season in 2016, and Coach Kelly was evaluating every facet of the program. Watching some of this take place in-person was an incredible learning opportunity. He met with just about every player in the program and sought feedback on their experience. He had uncomfortable conversations with leadership and wanted to know what he could do better. Then, he set in motion a plan to reset and refocus the culture of the program.

Coach Kelly began the movement within our football family to focus on the process of improving every day, established a series of traits that we were going to build upon

Working with a young person on a daily basis and watching that person grow and develop is incredible.

consistently, and created an atmosphere where coaches and staff were going to encourage self-determination in our players.

"Self-determination" theory grew out of the work of psychologists Edward Deci and Richard Ryan. They introduced it in their book *Self-Determination and Intrinsic Motivation in Human Behavior.* It references people's ability to make choices, manage their own lives, and remain motivated to action if they feel they have a direct effect on outcomes. Deci and Ryan believe three psychological needs must be met in order for self-determination to take place:

- **C**ompetence: People have to learn and gain mastery of the skills that are needed for success.
- **A**utonomy: People need to feel in charge of their own goals and behaviors.
- **R**elatedness: People need to feel a sense of belonging, community, and attachment to others.

Coach Kelly talks all the time about the need for the coaches and staff to drive the C.A.R. We have to teach the players the skills they need to win, give them autonomy, and build meaningful relationships with them. When we do this, we create an atmosphere where self-determination exists and the players will be motivated by journey itself and the satisfaction of improving.

Brian Kelly believes in building connections with his players. I have heard him tell recruits over and over, "I hire coaches to handle scheme. I am here to make sure that you are on able to achieve to the best of your ability, in every part of your life." I have watched him live this out as he emphasizes communication with the team and focus on their well-being. He has challenged me to think differently and change. I am a better coach because of it. The Fighting Irish football program was better off for it as well.

In the five years since hitting the reset button, we had some good success. Notre Dame won 54 games, finished the 2018 regular season 12-0, appeared in the 2018 and 2020 College Football Playoffs, and won two bowl games. The program also achieved at record-setting heights in the classroom. These things do not take place without refocusing on the relationships with our young people. That same success will follow Coach Kelly to LSU. We saw the foundation laid in 2022 when he took over a team that had only 39 scholarship players, transforming it into a unit that won 10 games, appeared in the SEC Championship, and won a bowl game. Relationship driven programs succeed anywhere in the country and in any conference. Coach Kelly's teams are proof of that.

CHAPTER 2

Why Relationships Are Important

Unfortunately, we are living in a time, when more and more young men and women feel disconnected. They are searching to find their place in the world around them, and they feel isolated and alone. Teens and young adults are battling anxiety, depression, and emotional/psychological distress at higher rates than ever before.

According to the Anxiety and Depression Association of America, anxiety disorders are the most common mental illness in the country. They effect 19 percent of the population, consisting of 40 million adults who are 18 years or older. According to the National Institute of Mental Health, 32 percent of adolescents between the ages of 13-18 suffer from anxiety, and 22 percent of young adults between the ages of 18-29 do, as well. An alarming number of high school and college age young adults are struggling with their mental health.

There is a rising sense of helplessness and despair amongst our children. Unfortunately, that despair has led to the highest suicide rate amongst U.S. teens and young adults since 2000. According to the *Journal of the American Medical Association*, in 2017 alone, suicide claimed the lives of 5,016 males and 1,225 females between the ages of 15 and 24.

The suicide rate for teen boys, specifically, has seen an alarming rise. According to 2017 data from the Centers for Disease Control (CDC), young men between the ages of 15 and 19 are committing suicide at a rate of 17.9 per 100,000. That is up from 13.0 per 100,000 in 2000. It's staggering to think about, but suicide is now considered to be the second leading cause of death for Americans between the ages of 10 and 43. In the span of just four years, I have witnessed two different players in crisis. One was a player on an active roster who attempted suicide and another was an alumnus who committed suicide only a couple of years removed from graduation. It is gut-wrenching and nearly impossible to comprehend.

There are any number of factors involved in why this is happening; some supported by research, and some are educated guesses. The ADAA states, "Anxiety disorders develop from a complex set of risk factors including genetics, brain chemistry, personality, and life events." There is little doubt that the opioid epidemic sweeping our nation is an element. The digitalization of our society and the pressures that come with social media play a role as well, as do simple things, such as nutrition, lack of sleep, and adequate exercise.

What we know is that a high percentage of young men and women across the country are having difficulties, and we have to support them. According to San Diego State University psychologist Jean Twenge, "I don't think it is an exaggeration at all to say that we have a mental health crisis among adolescents in the U.S." Generation Z is struggling.

Parents, teachers, administrators, and coaches—we are all on the front lines of this battle. We are the caretakers of our children, our students, and our players. It's our job, our responsibility, to help protect and develop our young people. We have to establish standards of performance and personal behavior and then hold them accountable to those standards. In order to do that, it is imperative that we understand how important relationships are, and we dedicate ourselves to building them with the same intensity and attention to detail that we apply when building fundamental skills in athletics!

Healthy relationships can lead to an overall healthier life. They are vital for our well-being as human beings and are often the glue that holds people together during difficult times. They provide stability and in turn, positively affect our emotional, mental, and physical lives. The benefits of having healthy relationships are many:

Healthy relationships are vital for our well-being as human beings and are often the glue that holds people together during difficult times.

❑ Less Stress

Having meaningful and committed relationships are linked to less production of the stress hormone, cortisol. Cortisol is a hormone that works with certain parts of the brain to control mood, motivation, and fear. This suggests that people who are a part of healthy relationships are less responsive to psychological stress. Also, the support that comes from those relationships serves as a protector against the stresses that life will inevitably present.

❑ Better Healing

Even a small amount of emotional support can go a long way in helping someone recover from a sickness, an injury, or a procedure. Having another person there to support you, remind you to take your medicine, to continue your rehab, or simply to take your mind off your situation can aid in recovery. It provides the patient with more confidence in their ability to handle their pain and recovery.

❑ Positive Behaviors

Healthy relationships set the tone for overall healthier lifestyles and choices. Young people are likely to model the positive choices made by parents, partners, teachers, coaches, and peers. If the people around the players are making good choices in regards to such things as diet, exercise, sleep, or drugs and alcohol, the players are more likely to follow their lead and make similar choices.

fizkes/Shutterstock.com

It is human nature for people to want to feel needed.

- [ ] Greater Sense of Purpose

As was mentioned earlier, it is human nature for people to want to feel needed, like they belong to something bigger than themselves. Student-athletes will strive to be the best version of themselves, if they feel like they are working on behalf of and for the unit or team. Just being with other people who have something in common contributes to well-being.

Strong, healthy relationships also allow young people the confidence to be their true selves. They provide the safety and security for our student-athletes to allow themselves to be vulnerable and not afraid to ask for help. In my experience, creating an atmosphere where our young men are not afraid to seek us out and look for help has been a major challenge in recent years. For young men, specifically, there seems to be a perception that asking for any kind of help, whether it be mental, emotional, social, academic, or athletic, is a sign of weakness. The foundation and maintenance of strong relationships helps erode this perception and allows us to do our jobs better, which is to support our athletes in every facet of their lives.

During my career, I have encountered numerous players who were afraid to ask for help and let me know that they were in some sort of difficulty. In some cases, I didn't have a clue what a young man in our program was dealing with, because he never showed any outside signs of distress. In other cases, it was clear something was amiss, because the general demeanor, the academic results, or the on-field performance was not up to standards.

In my first season as a head coach, I made the mistake of focusing only on the fact that the standard was not met. I would dwell on the actions and make sure to voice my displeasure. I learned very quickly to ask *why* the player was falling short of the standard. I wanted to know if there was something going on, away from the field, that was causing stress or anxiety.

"I have seen a couple of poor academic reports, you are not practicing well the last couple of days, and you don't seem like yourself. What's going on in your life right now that is causing you to be so out-of-sorts?"

I would guess that nearly 75 percent of the time there was something going on in that young man's life that was adversely affecting his ability to function day to day. I also learned that I couldn't solve a lot of these problems. But, what I could do was show I cared by being a good listener and then directing that player to the resources on campus that could support him.

Sometimes, it's a young man's parents who have decided to divorce, sometimes, it's the loss of a relative, sometimes, it's a volatile relationship with a significant other—there are any number of outside factors that might cause a player to struggle. We won't know until we ask and then listen with intention. And sometimes, there is no outside stressor. They are just falling short. When that happens, we simply remind them of the standard and help them work better to reach it.

Working hard to build the right kind of relationships also serves another, and very important, purpose. We are showing our young people *how to love* and *how to allow themselves to be loved!* In this day and age, that is more significant than ever. According to the US Census Bureau, over 19 million children in America live in a home without a father. That is more than one in four. Another five million will grow up in a home without a mother. Those statistics are shocking and only emphasize the importance that a coach can play in providing a strong role model in the lives of our student-athletes. We can never replace their parents, but we have to try and fill in some of the holes. Providing and modeling a healthy, loving relationship might be the most important gap we can try to bridge.

Some coaches struggle to connect with players, and others have a gift for it. One of the best I have ever seen was Randy Hart, a legendary defensive line coach, who worked at Iowa State, Purdue, Washington, Notre Dame, and Stanford. He has participated in 10 Rose Bowls in his career—one as player at Ohio State and nine as an assistant coach at Ohio State, Washington, and Stanford. In the history of that great game, only one person has ever appeared in more.

Randy and I were together at both Notre Dame and Stanford, and I grew very close to both him and his lovely wife, Linda. Randy and Linda had two sons of their

If we, as coaches, make a concerted effort to build and maintain relationships, we are going to get a team that is hard-wired to succeed.

fizkes/Shutterstock.com

Working hard to build the right kind of relationships also serves another, and very important, purpose—showing our young people how to love and how to allow themselves to be loved!

own, John and Jay, but he treated every guy he ever coached like he was one their own. Randy knew what was going on in the lives of his players. He had them at his house and fed them. Randy's players got to know Linda, and she was there to support them, as well. Because he was so invested in them, he could coach them *hard* and be demanding of them. Those defensive linemen didn't always like Randy, but they trusted him and knew he cared. Because of that, his guys took coaching, always played hard, and got results.

Another coach I worked with who was exceptional at connecting with players was Mike Bradeson from the Nevada staff. Mike spent his entire career on the West Coast, with stops at Boise, Cal, UNLV, and Nevada. The Bay Area in the Northern California was his sweet spot in recruiting. He knew every high school and junior college coach in the area. He also invested a great deal of himself into the prospects that he recruited. Mike was going to do everything he could to make sure that his recruits were cared for and given every opportunity to be successful.

When Mike and I went on the road together in our first year, we stopped in at every school that had a prospect. We also stopped into the schools of the current players on our own team who came from the area. Mike knew that I was not completely familiar with the backstories of every player we had from the Bay, because I had not been involved in their recruitment. He felt it was important for me to meet their coaches, teachers, and the influential people in their lives at home. He understood that the knowledge I could gain might help me build bridges with those players back on campus. He was right. Unfortunately, Mike passed away in 2019 after a battle with cancer. The out-pouring of support shown to his wife, April, and his son, Drew, from former players was incredible and captured just how impactful he was in the lives of the men he coached.

Recently, Brian Daboll, the head coach of the New York Giants, provided me a glimpse into some of the things that effective coaches do now. Brian and I were high school teammates at St. Francis High School, outside of Buffalo, NY, and have been friends since 1990. We were together at lunch in Baton Rouge one spring, and he stepped away for a minute to Facetime a player who was a proud LSU graduate. He simply wanted to let that guy know he was on campus and how much he enjoyed it. The whole conversation lasted less than two minutes. I didn't ask Brian about the call, I didn't need to. I have heard from coaching friends that Brian Daboll is demanding on his players, but they play hard for him, because they know he cares. They feel that way because of gestures like the one I watched. He took a minute to tell a player that he was thinking about him. That's it—that's all it was. But, those moments add up and help bind the player and coach together.

Some coaches might read all of this and think to themselves, "I didn't want to become a social worker or a surrogate parent. I got into this profession to compete and to win." I understand that sentiment, and for a time, shared one that was similar. And let's be clear, competition and striving to win is an important thing. In professional sports, it is the most important thing.

That said, in recent years, there has been an added focus on the *individuals* with whom we are working. Hall of Fame coach Marv Levy once said, "Systems don't win. People do." Coaches are beginning to better understand that we are not here to simply make our players better on the field, but we are also here to develop them as people, in every part of their lives. The beauty of that mindset, this attitude of servant-leadership, is that success and development on the field becomes a by-product. Focusing on people leads to winning!

In the business world, Google is at the forefront of understanding that the happiness of their employees has a direct effect on their bottom line. We have all read the stories about working at Google—the free food, the on-site dry cleaning, the gym, etc. Those perks are great, but it's much more than that. Google encourages their employees to have fun, allows them creative freedom, fosters a culture of trust, and exhibits values that are aligned across the organization. Because they invest in their workforce, Google is more successful.

Even if working hard to develop and model healthy, meaningful relationships is not in your comfort zone or speaks to your natural inclination, I would suggest that it should speak to your competitive nature as a coach. If we, as coaches, make a concerted effort to build and maintain relationships, we are going to get a team that is hard-wired to succeed. They will embody the traits that we are looking for from a winning team:

- They will feel better physically.
- They will be better equipped to handle adversity.
- They will make better choices, on and off the field.
- They will stick together and value team.
- They will seek out and accept coaching.

We are constantly trying to get our student-athletes to be the best version of themselves. We want this, because it is important for their development as people, and because it will put them in a better position to succeed on the field in competition. As coaches, we can only do that if we make building and modeling meaningful relationships a priority from the outset.

CHAPTER 3

The Building Blocks of Relationships

Professionals in the construction industry know that in order to create something lasting, there has to be a solid foundation. If we believe that relationships with our players are important, then we also must take the time to build a foundation from which healthy ones can grow and develop. This requires some very specific building blocks. A building block is defined as *something essential on which a larger entity is based*, and we must be sure that we are working to establish them in every relationship.

From my perspective, those building blocks are Trust, Time, Respect, Communication, and Love. Without these, a healthy relationship cannot truly exist. Like a building with a weak foundation, a relationship that is not based on these principles will most certainly crumble when under stress.

❑ Trust

When our players know that we respect them and that we will listen to them, we are building trust. Trust is an essential part of any healthy relationship, and it serves as a bonding agent between two people. Author Brian Tracy said, "Trust is the fundamental glue that holds any relationship together."

Trust is an abstract—you can't hold it in your hands. It is a feeling that is difficult to measure and put into degrees. We feel its presence—we know when it is there and certainly know when it is lost. As difficult as it is to quantify, it is impossible to truly connect with or reach another person without it.

When our players trust us as coaches, we are emboldening them to participate in relationships and be an active member of the team. Trust allows young people to contribute! If they learn how to trust their coaches and teammates: they will not hold back. When a player trusts the people around him, he is much less likely to limit his out-put. Trust encourages people to put themselves out there and leave their comfort zones, because it is their belief that the others around them will do the same. Trust between a coach and a player, or between teammates, can have a positive domino effect. It can create an atmosphere, where people aren't afraid to invest a great deal of themselves in the others around them.

Not only does trust empower young people to invest in relationships and put forth effort, it also enables them to handle adversity. In every interpersonal relationship, there are obstacles, times of difficulty. Trust allows people to work through those times instead of simply walking away. It's not easy to be challenged and to have your shortcomings pointed out. But, if you believe the person challenging you is looking out for your best interests, you are less likely to tune that person out. If the player trusts the coach and truly believes he's got his back, the player is more likely to allow himself to be coached.

Too many coaches believe that trust should just come with the job; it doesn't. Trust is earned over time and, often, in critical or difficult situations. I think back to every single time I joined a new program and started working with a new group of student-athletes. I understood that I had to earn their trust and never took for granted that I had it, just because I was wearing a whistle.

The first step in earning the players trust is being competent. That sounds like a simple concept, but you would be surprised how many coaches out there can't help their players get better. And the players know. If they feel that a coach doesn't know what he's doing and can't help them, there is no way the player is going to have any level of trust in that coach. Do you every wonder why in the NFL, a veteran player can trust and accept coaching from a person nearly his own age or some cases, even younger? Sean McVay was only 30 years old, when he became the head coach of the Los Angeles Rams. In his second season, he led them to an NFC Championship. In his fifth season and at the age of 36, he led the Rams to a Super Bowl title. His team obviously trusted him. That was because they knew, no matter how young he was, he could make them better. That's what matters most!

Another major step in earning trust as a coach is the willingness to hold oneself accountable. One of the quickest ways a coach can lose the trust of the players is by avoiding responsibility or dodging blame. It can't always be the players' fault. Many times throughout my career, I have heard head coaches or coordinators talk about how "the players weren't ready to play," or "they didn't execute well enough." The players

Not only does trust empower young people to invest in relationships and put forth effort, it also enables them to handle adversity.

hear those things and begin to think to themselves, "That guy will throw us under the bus in a heartbeat." Other times, coaches will stand up and say, "I did not have my guys prepared to play. I have to do better." The players hear that as well.

In week 10 of the 2019 NFL season, the Kansas City Chiefs lost to the Tennessee Titans 35-32 in a hard-fought battle on the road. Chiefs head coach Andy Reid opened his postgame press conference by saying, "I'll take responsibility for the loss." There are many reasons that Andy Reid is one of the most respected coaches in all of football; his players knowing that he will never sell them out publicly is one of them.

When times are difficult or at a critical point, coaches need to be at their best, because those are also the times when we can win the players over. There are always a couple of moments during the course of the year when things are going to be hectic. In those instances, if the coach can keep the players calm and help them to refocus, they know they have a coach they can count on. When things are at their most chaotic, the coach has to be the calmest. By doing so, he shows the players they have someone who is cool at the helm and can steer the ship during turbulent times. I'm not just talking about times on the field either. Turbulence shows up in many forms in the lives of young people, and we have to be there to help them navigate those times.

In my career, I think that I have been able to serve as a steadying force for players when they have dealing with difficulties away from the field or in their personal lives. There have also been moments during games when competition got the best of me. Those were missed opportunities and situations that I have learned from and hopefully won't repeat.

© Michele Sandberg/Icon SMI via ZUMA Press

There are many reasons that Andy Reid is one of the most respected coaches in all of football; his players knowing that he would never sell them out publicly is one of them.

As was stated previously, it takes time to build trust, and it can only take a moment to lose it, so value it. We also have to understand and appreciate the risk we are asking the players to take. We are asking them to depend on another person, and that can be very difficult for a lot of them to do. If we value the relationship with the player, as well as his trust, then, we have to work very hard to keep it. And when that trust between a coach and a player is strong, it is amazing what we can get accomplished together!

❑ Time

The single most important thing we can do for another person is make time for them. Time is the most valuable commodity that any of us have. It's one of the few things in our lives that we cannot buy. Therefore, we are going to invest our time in the things that matter most to us. It's really easy to *tell* someone that they are important to you. When we choose to share our time with someone, we are *showing* them that they hold an important place in our lives. We are showing them that they matter! And make no mistake—young people will not be fooled. You can tell them anything you want, but if you do not back those words up with action, they will see right through you.

The daily grind of this profession, or any profession for that matter, can be consuming. It can overtake our schedules and cause us to lose perspective. As coaches, we cannot allow that to happen. We have to make ourselves *available* to our players! I am shocked at how many coaches will not leave a meeting or get off a call, when a player comes to see them. If someone matters to us, we have to *make* time for them. Making time for another person is a sacrifice. We are giving up our own time and adjusting our own schedules for the needs of the player, and we must be willing to do this.

Brian Kelly, head coach at LSU, sets a very clear standard when it comes to prioritizing the people within the organization. If a player is looking for a coach and needs to visit, the coach is expected to step away from whatever it is he is doing and touch base with that young man. Sometimes, the issue is something really urgent, and sometimes it's not. What is most important though is that player knows he's important to his coach and that coach will stop what he is doing to spend time with him.

Clark Lea, the former defensive coordinator at Notre Dame and current head coach at Vanderbilt, is an incredible embodiment of this "players-first" attitude. He would break away from any meeting or stop his individual work, if a player needed to visit with him. Even in the heart of the season, Clark will give a young man whatever amount of time he needs. I have seen meetings like this take 90 minutes, yet Clark sets that time aside, without complaint. He does this knowing full well it will probably set his own schedule back, yet he does it anyway. For Coach Lea, the players are always the priority. I know, for a fact, that his defensive units recognized that sacrifice, and they appreciated him for it.

By giving of our time to others, we are building bonds. Those bonds are what keep groups together when things get hard. When those defensive players are in a difficult spot, whether it's in a game, a practice, or a lift, they are going to truly "hear" Coach Lea when he speaks to them. They will respond to him because they know, in their hearts, they matter to him.

When we choose to sacrifice time for others, we are also teaching. We are modeling the value of relationships for our players. We are showing them that if an individual holds an important place in our lives, we have to willing to make time for them.

❑ Respect

Without respect, we can never truly form a healthy relationship. Respecting another person means accepting them for who they are and what they believe, even if it is different from one's own beliefs. When we allow other people to be themselves, and to feel secure knowing that they will not be judged, we are showing them respect. If our players feel respected, they are more likely to express themselves openly, ask questions, and seek help when they need it.

How do we then show respect for people and still hold them accountable? Treating people with respect does not mean that we are afraid of conflict or of a difficult conversation. In fact, respect is major ingredient in productive conflict resolution. We can disagree and still show respect for one another. "Honorable people can disagree honorably."

The first way we work through conflict in a respectful manner is by making sure that we *listen* to our players and that we validate what they are feeling. Human beings are designed to be good listeners; we have two ears and one mouth. We should listen twice as much as we talk.

"I hear you, I understand what you are saying, and it is okay to feel that way."

When we tell a young person some version of "just get over it," we are showing that we don't respect them as people. We are telling them that what they are feeling is not important enough to us to talk about, and they should just move on from it. In reality, discussing the situation and trying to uncover the underlying issues should be the goal. The willingness to engage in that discussion is a sign of respect and should allow for a more productive solution. It should also allow us the opportunity to express how we feel and talk about what needs to be corrected.

Coaches hear players talk about their desire to be treated with respect all the time, and I absolutely agree with them. We should always remember to treat the student-athletes we work with the right way. And I also believe that a player should also feel empowered to discuss the situation, if he ever feels like he hasn't been treated properly.

Coaches are human too; we make mistakes. At some point, every coach is going to lose his cool or do a poor job of communicating his message. That said, there is a time and place to have those discussions and it is *not* on the field. I would tell our players all the time, you have every right to come talk with me, if you feel like I am wrong, but we just don't have time for it on the field. We have to keep working out there. Come see me after practice, in my office, and I will listen thoughtfully to everything that you have to say. I promise to give you all the time you need to express how you are feeling. We just don't have the opportunity for discussions on the field.

The next step in showing respect is acting and speaking with *honesty.* We owe the people that we care about honesty. One of the worst things a coach can do to a player is leave that person wondering how we feel about him or his performance. Telling someone the truth may not sound like a difficult thing, but it can be harder than you think.

Sometimes, we don't tell a player the truth, and we kid ourselves into thinking we are doing it to spare them and their feelings. In reality, there are times when we, as coaches, don't tell the truth because it takes the burden off us. Delivering bad news is not enjoyable, and it is not easy. It takes courage to tell someone that their role may never be what they want it to be or that they simply may not be talented enough. If the player/coach relationship is healthy, the player should know, without a doubt, his coach will always tell him the truth. He may not necessarily agree with what his coach has to say, but he will know that he is not being lied to.

I am reminded of this when I watch the show "Hard Knocks" on HBO every year. The network imbeds a production crew with an NFL franchise during their pre-season preparations. It is fascinating television. It is also an example of how difficult it is to tell the truth. Every year, they will show a GM or a head coach releasing a player from the team, and inevitably that coach will tell the player some version of, "It may not work out with us, but you are good enough to play in this league." In some cases that is the truth, but it a lot of cases it is not. It's just easier to say that than tell a guy that he should probably give up on his dream and begin to move on with his life.

Without respect, we can never truly form a healthy relationship.

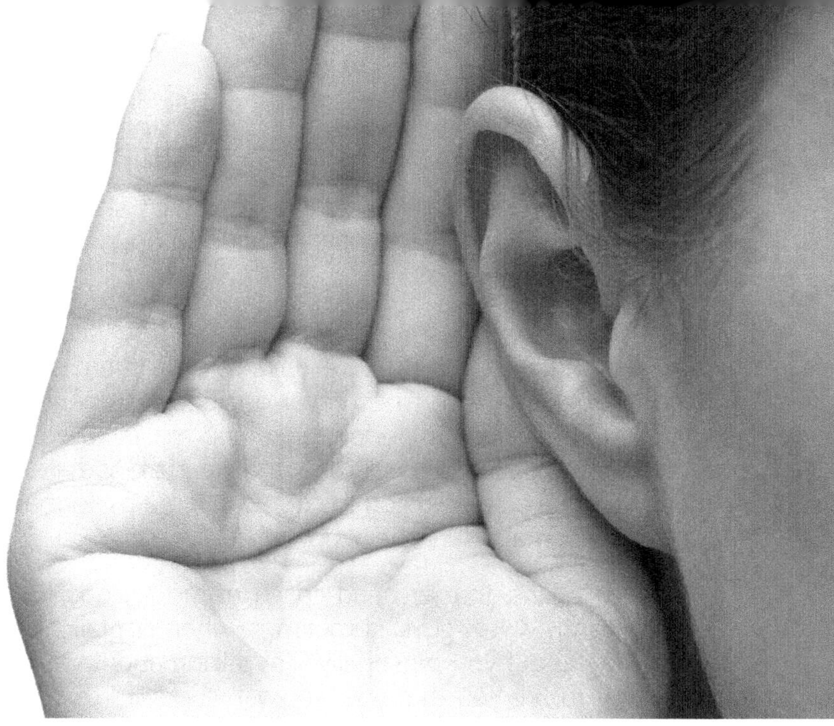

Voronin76/Shutterstock.com

The first way we work through conflict in a respectful manner is by making sure that we listen to our players and that we validate what they are feeling.

I think back to my own father, an executive in the NFL for over 30 years, and how his honesty helped me at a time when I needed it most. I was a slightly above-average high school football player at St. Francis High School, just south of Buffalo, NY. I had dreams of playing Div. I college football. I was also painfully undersized and slow. My dad was a professional talent evaluator; he knew full well that I could never play at that level. He sat me down and told me the truth. He told me to focus on Div. III programs and even then, playing college football was going to be a challenge for me. That was not an easy thing to hear, but it enabled me to focus on places where I would fit and, eventually, led me to John Carroll University. The decision to attend JCU was one of the best and most formative in my life. So much so, that I've returned to campus in a leadership role. I may not have found my "right place," if my father was not comfortable enough to tell me the truth. His honesty was a sign of respect and a symbol of his love for me.

As a coach, I was faced with this situation a lot, because I am a special teams coordinator. Those units are filled with a large cross-section of the football team. We utilized offensive and defensive players, we used starters and back-ups, and we used veteran and young players alike. From time to time, a non-scholarship player could carve out a meaningful role by playing in the kicking game. Those players are blast to work with because of how invested they are. However, it creates a scenario where other walk-ons want the opportunity to prove themselves as well. Culturally, that is a great problem to have. Unfortunately, not every player is physically capable of contributing. That is not an easy conversation to have, but it's certainly more honest and respectful than saying, "Just keep working hard, and your time will come."

Treating the players with the respect that they deserve, by listening and always being honest with them, does not mean that we can't coach them hard. It does not mean that we can't hold them to a high standard! We can, and should, coach them hard. We just have to pay attention to *how* we are doing it in order to keep the relationship healthy.

Coaches need to set a standard of performance with the players, and then hold them accountable to it. But we have to hold them accountable the right way. It can never be personal—we must never degrade a student-athlete under our care. We are charged with evaluating performance and making sure that it lives up to the standard. If that performance does not meet the standard, we are expected to point that out and then provide a plan of action to correct it. If the performance is not what we are looking for, we must make sure they know it!

Bruce Arians, former head coach of the Arizona Cardinals, once told his team in training camp; "New guys, sometimes, when I'm talking to you, it can get ugly. But I'm not talking about you personally—I'm talking about your football. If your football sucks, I'm going to tell you that your football sucks. I like you as a guy." There is probably a more gentile way of saying that, but it gets the point across. We are critiquing the football, not the person. As Coach Kelly likes to remind his staff, we can *"be demanding, without being demeaning."*

Coaching hard not only means pointing out when the standards aren't met, it also means celebrating the victories with the same intensity! Even the smallest victories need to be pointed out and celebrated. Whenever we can do that in front of player's peers, it is even more impactful.

During training camp, I kept a large bucket of snack-size candy at the front of the meeting room. If a player had a good rep in a drill or a good play in a team period, we rewarded them in front of the rest of the group with a piece of candy. Because the Milky Way bar is the greatest candy bar ever invented (my opinion), they were saved for the exceptional plays.

You would be surprised how fired up a group of guys will be for a snack-size bit of chocolate. They hoot and holler, when they see a big play on film and immediately begin to cheer for one another. "Coach—c'mon man, that has got to be worth a Milky Way!" By recognizing a job well done as often as we point out the mistakes, we are showing the players the respect we have for their effort.

❑ Communication

Communication is the basis of every relationship in our lives and should be worked on every day. We should always be able to talk comfortably with others, and if the topic is an uncomfortable one, we have to possess the ability to navigate through it. Kevin Sumlin, the former head coach at the University of Arizona and my boss at Texas A&M, told me once "leaders have to be able to have an uncomfortable conversation." Every year that I spend in athletics and working with young people, I am reminded of this.

Robert Kneschke/Shutterstock.com

Communication is the basis of every relationship in our lives and should be worked on every day.

In order to communicate clearly and comfortably, we must be able to be ourselves with no fear. I see this all the time in recruiting. A prospect will try to use words or phrases that they don't understand in order to impress a coach or a member of the media. I also see it from coaches who, out of nowhere, will develop an accent in order to try and find common ground with a recruit or a family. It's always a little funny when a coach from New Jersey suddenly speaks with a "southern drawl" in conversations with a prospect from Virginia! None of this stuff is necessary. To communicate with people confidently and clearly, we just need to be ourselves.

Styles of communication are very important as well, and this is a place where coaches have to learn to adjust. It is an area where I have spent time thinking about my habits and considering ways I can improve my approach to communicating with student-athletes, coaches, and staff.

I will occasionally use a four-letter word to make a point in a meeting. It's lazy and not something I am very proud of. My wife, Laura, will point out to me very quickly when those words are taking too prominent a place in my vocabulary. With that said, sometimes, it is effective to use the language of an 18- to 23-year old college student. It can be a little easier to help them understand the point. I will also get excited and raise my voice in those meetings. It helps to keep the players awake and alert and shows that my energy level is high. I have learned through experience that this kind of demeanor suits me best when celebrating a small victory or installing a concept. It is not nearly as effective, if I am making corrections, offering constructive criticism, or upset.

I am very lucky to call Tom Crean a friend and a mentor. His resume includes head coaching stints at Georgia, Indiana, and Marquette. In the late '90s, he was an assistant at Michigan State for Tom Izzo, at the same time, I was a GA for Nick Saban and the Spartan football program. We became friends, and he has been an important influence in my career.

A couple of summers ago, we had a long discussion about styles of communication, especially at times when things were not going well. We talked about how times have changed, as have the student-athletes, and that we had to adjust or we weren't going to be able to effectively communicate with the players. He offered some very specific tips from his own personal experience and how he had adjusted over the course of his career. He talked about being measured in his tone of voice, careful about his vocabulary, and making sure there was context to everything he said. I began to look critically at my own communication style and looked for ways I could improve.

When a play or a performance is not up to the standard we have set, I start by reminding myself to calm down. The first thing that I am going to do is lower my voice. That serves two purposes; first, it forces the players to focus on what I am saying in order to hear me. Second, it shows that while I am upset, I am also under control.

The next thing I am going to do is be very mindful of the words that I choose. I will never use foul language when I am making a serious correction or critique. I do not want the player's focus to be on abusive language; I want it to be on the coaching point being made. There is an old saying, "Focus on the message and now on how it's delivered." I don't think that applies anymore. If we want the players to hear the message, we can't *distract* them with how it's delivered.

Finally, like Bruce Arians, I decided I am never going to be critical of the person, only the performance. When a player feels like you are attacking him, there is very little chance that he is going to be receptive to the coaching point you are trying to make. If we are critical of the person, we put them on the defensive, and that is not where we want them to be. We also affect the overall atmosphere in the room. The players are going to look out for another. If they feel a peer is being treated poorly, they are not going to react well either. The best course of action is to calmly point out why the performance fell short of the standards and then provide a way for it to be corrected.

In the fall of 2019, Notre Dame played the University of Virginia in an important game at home. We were coming off of a difficult loss at Georgia the week before and had challenged the team to respond to the adversity. Both teams were ranked in the Top 25, the stadium was full on a brilliant fall afternoon, and millions watched on NBC television. It was a pivotal moment in the season. We won the game, but played very poorly on special teams. We allowed an onside-kick to be recovered, and we fumbled a punt, allowing UVA to have two extra possessions. We also missed a short field goal. It was not complimentary football. We did not hold up our end of the bargain in the kicking game; the offense and the defense had to pick us up.

I was angry and anxious before going into the Monday meeting with the players. Coach Kelly stopped into my office to visit, before I went downstairs. He wanted me to understand that this was an important moment. The players would be watching closely to see how I handled this performance. He reminded me to make sure that our guys understood what we put on film was not good enough, but to stay calm and to frame all of the corrections in relation to the standards that we had set for our football team. It was great coaching point, because it helped me re-focus before heading into the auditorium and addressing the team. Afterwards, Coach Kelly made a point to tell me he thought the meeting went really well. I appreciated the feedback, because improving my communication style in difficult meetings was important to me.

Our ability as coaches and leaders to communicate clearly and efficiently, adjust to the audience, and exhibit the right demeanor is paramount in building relationships with our people and becoming more effective teachers and motivators. It also something that we can work on constantly and learn lessons from others, in order to continue to grow and get better.

❑ Love

When thinking about building relationships, love can be a complicated subject for some people. There are times when the word alone can make a person uncomfortable, because they believe it denotes some sort of romantic connotation. In reality, we all have a number of different and meaningful relationships that are not romantic in nature. We all love people in our lives that we do not view in any romantic way. Love does not automatically equate to romance.

Another misconception about the concept of love is that it is an emotional state of being. Love is not a warm and fuzzy feeling that comes and goes—it is ingrained in our being. It is part of our make-up.

Think about this in terms of marriage. Not every husband and wife feels "in love" with their spouse every minute of every day. Those feelings can ebb and flow with the normal up and downs of daily interactions and conflict. Unconditional love is not dependent on how things are going between the two people in a relationship.

Love is, however, a deep sense of commitment that two people feel for one another. Commitment is not only a feeling—it is a feeling followed by action. It is that simple; love is action. Love is service to the people in our lives who matter the most to us.

When we recruit a player and then coach them on a daily basis, we are making a commitment to them. We are saying, "You are more important than me." Our commitment is to serve them, no matter how we are feeling about them at any particular moment. That doesn't mean we always have to like them, or that we cannot be mad at them from time to time. What is most important for the health of the relationship is that when we act, we act out of love. There is a promise being made to them that we will be consistent with our commitment. No matter what is happening in our lives or theirs, they can expect that we will always treat them with love. Love is a sacrifice, and our willingness to make that sacrifice cannot depend on how we are feeling on any given day.

Love also means setting standards and holding people accountable to them. I truly believe that *discipline is an expression of love*. Sometimes, that can feel like a conflict. How do I keep telling my players that I love them and then enforce the rules, which can sometimes have some serious ramifications?

To truly love a player is to help prepare them for life beyond school and athletics. That is acting in their best interests. In the larger world, when people break the rules, there are consequences. In the same way that parents introduce that concept to their children, we have to reinforce it with our players. If you screw up, there is a price to pay. When it is over, it is over. No matter what, we will never stop loving you.

Unfortunately, headlines from across the country describe systematic failures in leadership. Too often, we see athletes fall short of standards with little or no consequences. Turning a blind eye to serious crimes or violations of personal dignity does not help a player or a program. Winning is great and is a must, but not at the expense of lowering the standards. That only hurts the players in the long run.

Any good program is built on a foundation of principles and beliefs. When things get tough, those programs always revert back to what it is at their core. Relationships are no different. If we want them to be healthy, meaningful, and lasting, they have to be built on *Trust, Time, Respect, Communication,* and *Love*.

CHAPTER 4

How to Build Better Relationships

Now that we have established a good foundation, we have to work consistently to build our relationships and make them stronger. In order to accomplish that, we have to seek opportunities to interact with other people. If we are always holed up in our offices, looking at video, where and when are we going to find the chances to learn about our players? If we are serious about developing bonds with our team, we have to be intentional about spending time with them. We have to go out of our way to be around the players and engage them in conversations. We have to be great listeners and show genuine interest in them beyond the field. Building a strong relationship does not happen by accident, it happens because both sides invest in the other.

The first thing that we have to remember about relationships is that they are two-way streets. There has to be give and take. No one person can dominate a healthy relationship!

In order for a relationship to be meaningful, there must be mutual interest in one another. Coaches can fall prey to this from time to time. Sometimes, when we share what it going on in our lives with a player, we feel as though we are connecting with them. By only talking about the things that interest us or happen in our own lives, we are making the dynamic one-sided. For example, sitting with a player at lunch and asking, "Hey, have I told what's happening with my daughter lately?" That question doesn't show genuine interest in the other person, and it won't help us learn anything new about them. We have to be willing to ask other people about themselves and what is happening in their lives, because then, we gain insight into who they are as people and show them that we are interested.

I learned this lesson with Brandon Garcia, a player who finished his career at Notre Dame in 2019. He was a walk-on, defensive back from Seton Catholic Prep in Chandler, Arizona. He was a stereotypical Notre Dame walk-on—a tremendous student who majored in neuroscience and behavior, started his career in inter-hall football on campus, and worked his tail off at practice every single day on the scout team.

Brandon appeared in one game his entire career, on senior day versus Boston College. I passed him once in a hallway and stopped to ask him about a tattoo he had on the inside of his forearm. He had the outline of a bicycle in thick, black ink. He told me it was in honor of his late-grandfather, who had been an important influence in his life. His grandfather had taught him how to ride a bike and that's why he selected the artwork. Brandon spent a couple of minutes telling me all about his grandfather and his family. That simple question got him talking about his life away from our building and helped me gain insight into who he is as a person. That small investment for me resulted in a big return in regards to our relationship.

It is not just the coaches either. The athletes themselves can also fall into one-sided relationships. They get very used to talking about themselves and fixating on their own worlds. Like us, they do not think to ask about others. We see this in the dynamics that exist between players and coaches, staff, and even their own teammates. If we are going to stress the importance of relationships in the organization, then we also need to educate everyone what a healthy relationship looks like. Then, as coaches, we need to model it.

Simply stated, we must be interested in and know the details of our players' lives. In college athletics, a lot of this learning takes place during the recruiting process. We engage in conversations and try to learn as much as we can about each individual. What are their interests away from sports, what type of personality do they have, what is their family life like, what do they want from their future? These are all important questions, among many others, and we are asking them so that we can get to know each prospect better. We are also trying to understand the challenge(s) that each guy faces.

A football team is just a smaller sampling of society. All the same struggles that families face in the real world present themselves on a football team. Socio-economic differences, drug and alcohol abuse, physical and mental disabilities, family dynamics—we see all of it.

A football team is just a smaller sampling of society.

Experience has taught me just about every young person faces some sort of serious challenge in their life. It doesn't matter if it was at Texas A&M, Stanford, Notre Dame, LSU, or John Carroll. They just look different from individual to individual. We have to be able to identify those challenges in order to truly understand the person.

During the recruiting process, our interest in the lives of the prospects is motivated by the fact that we want to build a bond with them, so that they will choose our university and play for our program. Once they arrive on campus, our interest in their lives should not wane. Too many college coaches fall into this trap. Once a recruiting cycle is complete, their focus then shifts to the next class, and they lose sight of the people that have just joined their family. In order to continue to build those relationships, we have to remain curious about our players. Most of the time, there is a whole lot more we can learn about a person, after the recruiting process is finished.

Knowing the details of each player's life can sound like a daunting task. For a position coach, it really shouldn't be that bad. The numbers in each group are usually manageable. For the coordinators, it could be a little bit more difficult to know something about every player on their side of the ball. Position coaches can help the coordinators and provide them some information or reminders about each guy. For the head coach, knowing the details of the lives of over 100 student-athletes in the program can be difficult, if not impossible. Sometimes, it takes a little creativity and a little homework for the head coach to learn about his roster.

Jim Hofher, whom I consider a dear friend and mentor, kept a notebook when he became the head coach at the University at Buffalo. It contained a headshot and some bio information on every member of the team. He would set aside some time each night to study that binder and try and learn something about each guy. I noticed that, and I also noticed how it positively impacted the players. They appreciated that when Jim engaged them, he already knew something about them individually. Little things like this take some extra effort, but they go a long way in showing your team that you are interested in them not only as athletes, but as people too.

Matt House, the defensive coordinator and linebackers coach at LSU, is also great at this. When he arrived in Baton Rouge, he stayed in the office well into the evening for the first couple of weeks spending one-on-one time with each player on defense. It was not unusual to see a line form outside of his office, because his conversation with a guy was running long. The players took note of that, and it was not surprising to see how quickly he built bonds with the young men on his side of the ball.

I personally believe that a coach should work intentionally to connect with every single player with whom he interacts. However, this is not for everyone. If it's not in your nature or comfort zone to build relationships with big cross section of people, think pragmatically. If you want to be successful, you must invest in and know about the lives of your *best players*. That statement may not be in-line with the overall theme of this book, and I understand that, but there are reasons behind it.

First and foremost, your best players have the ability to affect winning and losing, which at the college level determines whether or not you can keep your job. By working hard to build and maintain strong relationships with your best people, you are hopefully putting them in position to be their most productive. That is good for everyone. Also, by putting effort into connecting with them, the more likely you are to keep them. In this day-and-age of student-athletes transferring without a second thought, trying to build bonds with your most talented players is an investment in player-retention.

The best players on a team are usually the tone-setters in the locker room. It is not always the case, but in most instances, your best players are going to exert some sort of leadership and bring others with them. When one of your most productive guys is not on board with the coaches, that person can become an energy-vampire and suck the positivity right out of the room. By going out of your way to build bonds with the best players, hopefully, you can influence them to bring the team along in the right direction. If your best people are living up to the standards and modeling the values that you want for the program, the more likely that culture is to take hold throughout the team in general.

In football, we see the players a great deal during the season. We really don't have to go out of our way to find opportunities to spend time with them. It is a little bit more difficult in the off-season, but not impossible, because they are in the building throughout the course of the week. When they are on a break or when we are away from campus is when it is most challenging, and when we really have to make a concerted effort to stay connected to the players.

There are so many different opportunities to engage with our athletes, and we should take advantage of all of them. The following are some ways to better connect with our young people:

❑ Pre- and Post-Practice

Have you ever noticed the coach who walks through the stretch lines, before and after practice, and is talking to players? While other coaches congregate and talk to one another, the coach walking the lines is taking advantage of a great opportunity to get a "touch" on a number of different players. In moments like these, we can share a joke, offer a coaching point, or simply just check-in with one of the players. These "touches" add up after a while and offer the chance to get to know players with whom we would not normally have much interaction. Smart coaches take advantage of these moments and use them to build rapport with a large cross-section the team.

❑ Locker Room

Spending time in the locker room with the players is a new concept for me. There was a time that I treated the player's locker room as a sacred space that belonged to them. I always assumed they didn't want to see the coaches in there anyway. I have changed my thinking on this now, because the locker room is a relaxed atmosphere, where they will let their personalities show.

At LSU and at Notre Dame, I would go into the locker room 20 minutes before every special teams meeting and just hang out. You would be surprised at what the players are willing to share with you, how much you can learn by watching them interact with one another, and frankly just how funny they are. Chris Finke, former WR and captain for the Irish, used to write a question of the day on the white-board next to his locker. For example: "Are there more chairs or people in the world?"—"What is your favorite Thanksgiving side dish?"—"When you wipe your bottom, do you wipe from behind or from underneath?" (That one was a personal favorite of mine. Only college guys could come up with that.) These polls, while clearly non-scientific, would sometimes generate some heated discussion, a lot of laughter, and would get a wide swath of the team involved in the conversation. I looked forward to coming down every day and seeing what Chris had come up with for that afternoon.

❑ Meeting Room

The meeting room in another great place to get to know your players, as well as a great place for them to get to know one another. There are often a number of guys who will arrive early, take their seats, and just relax and get settled before a meeting begins. I enjoy listening to them talk to each other at these moments. This is especially fun to listen to early in training camp, as the veterans pepper the new guys with questions. In a special teams meeting, the players are spending time with guys from other position groups. They have a chance to get to know a guy with whom they don't normally spend a ton of time. Matthew Smiley, the special teams coach for the Buffalo Bills, will close his Friday afternoon by picking a player and asking him to share with the group, "The best and worst things that happened this week." In the NFL, it is not unusual to bring in new players throughout the course of the season, so Coach Smiley tries to use a minute in his meeting room as an opportunity to get the new guys comfortable and to learn something about them. It's a great idea.

The meeting room is also a great place to try and continue to build the culture of your unit, your side of the ball, or your team. By taking a couple of moments at the beginning or end of a meeting to show our guys that we are serious about them as people, we continue to emphasize and model the value of relationships. On Thursdays during the season, if we had won the previous game, I would provide doughnuts in the special teams meeting. I wanted to show the players a small token of my appreciation for their effort.

We would also provide the guys an opportunity to show each other the same appreciation. To begin that Thursday meeting, we opened with "Tell your teammate you love him." The guys would stand up, walk all over the room, hug each other, and express their gratitude. It became a tradition and one that I really enjoyed. I find it amazing, the way the players embraced one another and expressed their gratitude.

I was humbled when they would come up to me, put me in a bear hug, and say, "I love you, coach." It usually lasted so long, we would have to flash the lights in the room to get the guys to go back to their seats.

❑ Training Room

The training room is a little trickier, because it is a working area, and the medical staff has little interest in people loitering in their area. However, I know it is meaningful to walk through and check in with the student-athletes who are injured.

It's natural for a player who is hurt to feel removed from the team. When coaches are coming through the treatment area to check in on them and to offer encouragement, it matters. We are showing the player that we care about him, no matter what. Our interest in him is not dictated by his availability to play.

Also, it always good to check in with the training staff and say hello to them. Again, building relationships is important across the board, not just with the athletes. The support staff needs to know that we appreciate them as well.

❑ Weight Room

This is an area where no long, in-depth conversations are going to take place. In every weight room in the country, there is usually some high-tempo, high-intensity work going on. And it is usually very loud!

Just the coach's *presence* alone in the weight room is meaningful. When the players see that we are with them, and interested in what they are doing away from the field, it is a connection point. We are also emphasizing the importance of the strength and conditioning work that they are doing in there. When a guy has a great set or reaches a personal best, and his coach is right on the spot to offer positive feedback, it is impactful.

The weight room is also an opportunity to learn more about how our players take coaching from someone other than ourselves. We get a chance to see how they react to the strength staff and to their peers in physically taxing situations. The more insight we gain, the better we can connect with and coach them.

❑ Meals

Sitting down and having a meal with a student-athlete is a great opportunity to get to know them. Sharing a meal allows for conversations to take place. It is relaxed setting, and we can ask questions as simple as "How are you doing?" or "How was your day?" and see where they take us.

The weight room is also an opportunity to learn more about how our players take coaching from someone other than ourselves.

In the Polian household, my wife, Laura, will ask our children for their "Pit and Peak," as we sit for dinner. She wants to hear what they thought was the worst part and the best part of their day. It can be astonishing where the conversation can go from there. Just being together at the same table offers us a chance to stay connected with the people we care about.

❑ Outside the Facility

Technology becomes a bigger part of the equation, when our players are away from the building. Obviously, phone calls are great, but text and DMs are really valuable, as well. The "group text" that is set up by position is a great way not only to keep the coach connected with his players, but also to keep the players connected to one another. It can also be a great source of comedy. I am always amazed at how witty and sharp these guys are when they are teasing one another.

Handwritten notes are incredibly valuable as well. Dropping someone a note has become a lost art in this day and age of e-mail, text messaging, and DM's. Taking the time to write someone a quick card is a great personal touch that we can use as coaches. When I was at Nevada, I wrote every player in the program a card before they went home for the summer break. I just wanted them to know that I was grateful for the opportunity to be their coach and thank them for their work. I have also seen coaches at LSU and Notre Dame hustle down to the locker room after practice and leave a note for a player in his locker. Players appreciate it, when we take the time. And getting a handwritten note is a little unusual for them, so it has an impact.

With all of that said, we do have to pay attention to *how* we are engaging them. If every single conversation focuses on football, they can get the impression that we only care about them as players, and not as people. We never want our guys to feel like they are commodities. As coaches, we have to find ways to meet them "where they live."

CHAPTER 5

Consumer Relationships vs. Covenant Relationships

Initiating relationships with players is pivotal to our ability to connect with them and help them develop, as is establishing them on a solid foundation. That said, not all relationships are the same, and we have to make sure that we are working to build the *correct type* of relationships, and we are doing it with every young person with whom we work.

In early 2020, my wife, Laura, and I attended Sunday services at Granger Community Church in our hometown of Granger, IN. GCC is a Methodist church that was founded in 1986 by Pastor Mark Beeson and had been my wife's home church, since we returned to Notre Dame in 2017. I am a practicing Catholic, so there are times when we attend service together and times when I will attend mass on my own. On this particular Sunday, I decided to attend with her.

GCC is a wonderful place. It is filled with good people who serve one another and their communities. The music is incredible, the children's program is terrific, and there is a true feeling of fellowship the moment that you walk in the building. I recognize all of these things, yet I have difficulty at times getting comfortable there.

When you are born and raised Catholic, as I was, a non-denominational worship service is a departure from the tradition and familiarity of the mass. The music alone is so foreign. I am used to singing along from a hymnal, as a chorus leads the congregation with the help of a piano or an organ accompanying them. The opening fifteen minutes at GCC will feature a full band, lights, and multiple singers. The rites of the mass are comforting in some ways—the kneeling, the smell of the incense, and the praying in unison. It all reminds me of my youth, and it is all so familiar. There are times that I struggle with GCC, not because it is not a great place, but mostly because it is just different for me.

I am very grateful that Laura, or divine intervention, brought me to GCC this particular Sunday, because I heard a message that completely changed the way I looked at coaching and the way I approach relationships with players. Dr. Bob Laurent was only five minutes into his sermon, when I reached into my pocket and pulled my phone out, so that I could start typing notes.

Dr. Laurent was introducing us to the concept of *Consumer vs Covenant Relationships*, an idea that had originated from pastor and author Timothy Keller. He was talking about these two different types of relationships, as they related to marriage, and more importantly, to God. I followed his line of thinking and understood exactly the point he was trying to make. However, my mind went directly to our student-athletes, and to the relationship that a coach shares with a player. It became very clear to me how it could be applied to coaching.

❑ Consumer Relationships

We live in a consumer-driven society, where we are constantly trying to find the newest upgrade or the best deals possible. Many of our decisions then become based on what is best for us individually and what makes us feel good at any given point in time. Our personal desires take precedence over everything else. Unfortunately, that attitude, that selfish line of thinking, has crept its way into how we treat and value our relationships.

A consumer relationship is one-sided. It works out of the mindset that the other person in the relationship must adjust to me and meet my needs, or I am going to leave the relationship for someone who can. The whole relationship is centered around our desires and what we expect to gain from the other. We say, "I will be who I am supposed to be, as long as you are who you are supposed to be." The only goal in the end is my own fulfillment, no matter how we go about it.

The term "consumer relationship" is fitting, because that is the best way to illustrate it's meaning. I like the Jimmy John's chain of sandwich shops. I am in a consumer relationship with them. I order the #11, the Country Club. It has ham, turkey, provolone, lettuce, tomato, and mayo. I don't like the tomatoes, and I ask the server to hold them every time I order my food. As long as Jimmy John's keeps holding the tomatoes and getting my order right, I will continue to visit their store and pay them for their services.

OtmarW/Shutterstock.com

Not all relationships are the same, and we have to make sure that we are working to build the correct type of relationships, and we are doing it with every young person with whom we work.

If they get it wrong once, I will peal the tomato off of the sandwich and go about my lunch. If they get wrong twice, I might make a fuss and complain about it. If they keep getting it wrong, I'm going to end the relationship and take my business somewhere where they are going to get it right and meet my specific needs. This is the definition of a consumer relationship—my desires are more important to me than the relationship itself. The focus is on what I stand to gain, as opposed to what I can give.

The consumer relationship has an eroding effect on trust as well. If Jimmy John's keeps getting my order right, my trust in them will grow. If they start to get it wrong, my trust in them begins to decrease. The level of trust in the other person in the relationship is tied directly to performance. That is an unhealthy, and in some ways, unrealistic view of trust.

As we apply the consumer relationship mindset to something like ordering your lunch, most people would not consider it unreasonable. When we are paying for a sandwich, we should get what we asked for. Where we get into trouble is when we apply that consumer mindset to the interpersonal relationships we have with the people in our lives that matter to us.

Now, think about this in terms of a marriage. I vow to remain committed to my wife, provided she continues to work out and stay in shape. I am going to trust my wife, as long as she accepts the role of homemaker, as I envision it. The moment she does not live up to these expectations, I lose my trust in her and begin to think about removing myself from the marriage, because she is not meeting my needs and desires. From this point of view, the consumer relationship is flawed and dangerous.

If you flip the perspective and look at it from my wife's point of view, she is now in a marriage that is performance-driven. She is always going to feel pressure to meet my expectations. Inevitably, her performance is going to fall short at some point, and then, she will feel some version of guilt or shame, knowing that she was not good enough for me.

In any healthy relationship, there must be transparency and honesty. However, in a consumer relationship, those things cannot exist, because the fear of not measuring up is too great. The relationship will be superficial and lack depth. If my wife knows that she is constantly being measured on her performance, she will never allow herself to be totally vulnerable and possibly expose her faults. She will live in fear that the discovery of those shortcomings will cause me to leave the relationship.

A consumer relationship is not committed and is certainly not based in service to others. It lacks honesty, and it lacks trust. It is transactional, and there is no way any relationship with another person can be transactional in nature and still be considered healthy and meaningful. A consumer relationship is a version of "conditional love." And who has ever sought out and grown from conditional love?

❑ Covenant Relationships

The definition of a covenant as it relates to religion is an agreement that brings about a commitment between God and his people. Obviously, this was the focus of the Dr. Laurent's sermon. He applied this concept to the vow we take before God in marriage. Again, not only did I see it from that perspective, I also saw it in terms of the vow that coaches take to love the young people who are under our watch.

A covenant relationship is not selfish in nature. It is "other-centered." It is the acknowledgment that my partner in the relationship is more important than me. It focuses on what we have to give to the other person, and not what we can gain from them. It is a voluntary, mutual, binding promise to be loving, dedicated, and faithful, with no consideration to what the circumstances are.

In a covenant relationship, we say, "I will always be who I am supposed to be, whether you are being who you are supposed to be or not." It is a solemn vow to hold up your end of the deal, no matter what the other person does.

In this type of relationship, both parties have value and both parties are viewed as equals. That does not mean that we don't have roles to play. A husband may be the breadwinner and the wife the homemaker, and there is nothing wrong with that, as long as both are treated with equal respect. A coach can be the teacher and the player the pupil. As long as both are viewed as equally important in the relationship, it can be healthy and meaningful.

In a covenant relationship, both people are saying that the relationship itself is more important than any individual's desires. Both parties are committing to the other person and the other person's needs, even if mine are not being met.

The beauty of this kind of relationship is that it allows both people to be comfortable. They can drop their guard and be themselves. They can do this, because there is no fear that the other person is going bail at the first sight of failure or flaw. In fact, it allows us to be truly known to the other—known for all the good things, but also for all the negative things as well.

Religion has taught us the meaning of a covenant relationship through God's vow to love and care for us, no matter what we do. Religious love is universal, and salvation is open to all, despite our continued failure. Husbands and wives have shown us the meaning of covenant relationships by vowing to love one another "in sickness and health, and for richer or poorer." Friends display this relationship by dedicating themselves and serving one another, with no interest if it that service will ever be reciprocated.

A covenant relationship isn't a sign of love; it is the embodiment of love. You are voluntarily giving of your time, of your freedom. You are investing in others with no concern for their investment back. Covenant relationships are "unconditional love," and they are the most joyful and life-changing that we can experience in our lives.

Tymonko Galyna/Shutterstock.com

A covenant relationship is a sign of love; it is the embodiment of love.

❑ Coaching Should Be a Covenant Relationship

As the pastor was describing the consumer versus covenant relationship, it became immediately clear to me that the entire conversation applied to the coaching profession and the relationship dynamic between coach and player. My mind shifted easily to my favorite players from years past. I thought about how important those relationships were to me personally, how proud I was of all the things those men had accomplished, and the gratitude I felt for having been a small influence in their lives.

Just as quickly, my thoughts shifted to the athletes with whom I had difficulty. In that moment, I realized that I had failed them. I remembered back to all the times my attitude toward a player was dictated by his production on the field. I thought of the instances where I grew really frustrated with a young man, because he couldn't keep his life straight off the field. I was embarrassed as those specific names and faces kept popping into my head. That's when it occurred to me. Coaches need to make a conscious effort to treat *every* relationship with a player as a *covenant* relationship.

The strength of the bonds with our players cannot be dictated by their production as athletes. One of the worst possible lessons we can teach a child or young adult is that their value as a human being is tied directly to what they can or cannot do on a playing field.

As coaches, we can tend to use the performance of our position group, our unit, or our team as means to validate our own worth. We are trying to build a reputation as one of the finest coaches in the country. We seek notoriety from the media and the fan bases. Each year is a step closer to a more lucrative contract, as we measure ourselves in dollars and cents. The climb up the professional ladder never ends, and we are always looking for the next, bigger and better opportunity. All the while, we are investing our time, our energy, and our love into the players who *can help* get us where we want to go. And we are failing the ones who *can't.* Our needs and desires as coaches cannot be more important than the relationships we have with the players.

We are dealing with young people in the hallways of high schools and on college campuses. They are at a critical point in their growth. They are transforming themselves in terms of their mental, emotional, and physical development. In the best of circumstances, their lives are hectic. In the worst, their lives are turbulent. The longer one is in athletics and/or education, the more hardship and struggle we witness.

We have had guys on our teams dealing with adversity that I can't imagine dealing with as adult, let alone as a college student. Coaches need to be a steadying and consistent force in their lives. Our student-athletes *must* know that we are going to be the same, no matter who they are, what they have going on in their lives, or how they are performing. That is the vow a coach has to share with his player. "I have your back, and I will always have your back, no matter what."

When I look back over my career, and specifically to the early years as a head coach at Nevada, I am struck by how quickly I could lose patience with a player whom I did not view as a contributor. If a down-the-line player ended up in my office, because something needed to be addressed, I would often be short with him. I would make it very clear that whatever the issue was, the expectation was that it would get fixed immediately. If a starter was in my office for a similar reason, I found myself calmer and more willing to hear what they had to say. That's not what we are striving for.

Courtesy of Nevada Athletics

Healthy relationships can lead to an overall healthier life.

We never want the players to say that a coach has two sets of rules—one for the guys who help him win and another for the guys who don't see the field. Thankfully, we had a couple of senior leaders who had the courage to speak truth to power and came and expressed their frustrations with me. Obviously, I was learning as a first-time head coach and made some poor choices. Like players, coaches too grow from mistakes. I listened to what they had to say and worked very hard to make sure that I was as consistent as I could possibly be, with every player on the roster. There is no doubt that the culture around our program improved after the first season, because my staff and I committed ourselves to treating *all* the players with the concern, care, and respect that they deserved.

As the culture around the program evolved, a funny thing happened along the way. All of a sudden, a lot of the players who weren't performing up to expectations began to develop and blossom. Looking back on it, I am convinced that the consistency and the care that we showed them was a contributing factor in their growth. They were not afraid to try and not afraid to fail, because they knew the coaches were going to stay with them. Some of the least-gifted players, guys who were simply never going to be talented enough to play every down, began to carve out roles and make contributions. This happened because they felt valued and, in turn, gave great effort and found a way to help.

During this period, we also began to talk about how important relationships were to our team in general. We spoke openly about *loving* one another and valuing every opportunity to be together and share in each other's lives. That attitude grew within the team. Looking back on it now, the team was developing *covenant relationships* inside the locker room; I just didn't know to identify that way at the time.

This focus on the importance of relationships and loving one another sustained our Nevada team through one of the most difficult times many of us had ever faced in our lives. When we lost our teammate with the passing of Marc Ma, our players grew closer together as they supported each other after that tragedy. As the injuries in the 2016 season began to accumulate, the team did not fracture, and they didn't feel sorry for themselves. Finally, as the negativity surrounding the season began to increase, they closed ranks and hung together. I have never been so proud to be associated with a 5-7 year or more impressed with a team in my career.

That group of young men and those coaches/staff came together through tragic loss and incredible adversity. As things got tougher, they grew closer. It was incredible to hear the players say, "I love you" to one another. As they filed in for team meetings toward the end of the year, guys would walk up and down the rows and fist-bump or high-five their brothers. The coaches were focused on the players and making sure they understood how grateful we were for the way they were competing. That team battled at the end of that season, when a lot of other programs would have just mailed it in. That does not happen without a group of people making a vow to dedicate themselves to one another, no matter what is going on around them.

It's very difficult to look at a losing record and deem a season a success. Ultimately, coaches are judged by winning and losing, and we did not win enough. However, the journey of the 2016 Nevada football team taught me a very valuable lesson; love is an important ingredient for any program, and love can only grow if we make building relationships important.

As I mentioned earlier, the exploration of *consumer* versus *covenant* relationships spoke to me as a coach. I think there are some direct comparisons between applying this concept to a marriage and applying it to a player/coach dynamic. However, there is one characteristic of the covenant relationship that I struggle with, as it relates to working with young people.

One of the difficulties I face when thinking about coaching as a covenant relationship is the concept that *both* parties make a pledge to put the other person first. I think that is unrealistic, when you factor in the other person in our relationship is an adolescent or young adult. High school or college-age kids simply aren't thinking about relationships in those terms. Most are just trying to make it through the day and do the best they can.

There are some young people we work with who will naturally develop covenant relationships with those closest to them, because they are wired that way. They are selfless by nature, trusting of others, and open to relationships of all kinds. We are lucky to get to coach kids like that. Others, however, will always have some level of apprehension, when it comes to trusting coaches or teachers. That said, we can never change our approach to the young people who are not ready or capable of forming a covenant relationship with us. We have to enter into *every* relationship with the attitude that we are going to serve that person and place their needs in front of our own. It is the vow that we take.

Through all these years, I have learned that the trappings of winning come and go. Bowl rings, local celebrity, money—it is all fleeting. What sustains us, as coaches and teachers, over long careers, are the relationships. And when we enter into those relationships with a covenant mindset, they become some of the most valuable and fulfilling of our lives.

CHAPTER 6

The Dynamics of Diversity and Inclusion on Relationships

Throughout the process of thinking about and taking on this project, I asked myself if a book about the importance of relationships in coaching and teaching Generation Z should have a chapter dedicated to navigating race within the dynamics of those relationships. The answer was yes, it should. There are too many serious conversations going on across our world that are causing people to think and self-reflect about equality and inclusion. It would have been disingenuous to ignore them. In reality, you could dedicate an entire work to the subject. Speaking honestly though, I did not feel like I could address it without some help.

Over the course of a couple of months, I had multiple conversations with current and former players. My experience with these players literally spanned over decades and multiple universities throughout my career. The conversations were frank. There were players who shared with me where they felt like we had succeeded, as well as times where they felt like I fell short. They also shared areas where they felt like the programs or universities themselves could have done more to support their minority athletes. I admired the strength it took for these men to talk about such a difficult subject, and I listened with intent.

I sought out other coaches as well, from football and a handful of other sports too. In most cases, these coaches had been athletes at the college level and offered a unique perspective on how better to understand the experience of minority players. They knew both sides of the relationship intimately. Ultimately, I wanted to talk with and learn from people who could challenge and then help guide my thinking about how the dynamics of diversity and inclusion effect a player/coach relationship.

Like many others, tragedy sparked my thoughts about the dynamics of race. On May 25, 2020, George Floyd, a 45-year-old black man, was arrested and detained in Minneapolis, Minnesota for allegedly trying to pass a counterfeit bill. A police officer knelt on his neck for over eight minutes, while Floyd pleaded for help and onlookers filmed the incident. George Floyd was killed while in police custody, and millions of people watched through social and mainstream media. His senseless death ignited outrage across the country and throughout the world. Protestors took to the streets in cities across America to make their voices heard, forcing people to pay attention to and acknowledge the racial discrimination and inequalities that exist in our society.

On the Notre Dame campus, I took notice of the reactions by administration, Coach Kelly, the staff, and most specifically, the members of the team. Shortly after the protesting began, and the calls for social justice grew louder and louder, Coach Kelly held a team meeting. Due to the pandemic, he had to conduct it via Zoom. He asked the players to share their feelings and personal experiences. He wanted anyone who wished to speak, to do so honestly and from their hearts. He also encouraged them to use their platform as college football players to share their thoughts and insights with the public. In fact, he offered the services of the Notre Dame Football creative team and the program's social media outlets to amplify their voices. He gave the team an audience of hundreds of thousands to express themselves. That stood in stark contrast to some other places across the country.

The players' response was tremendous. They spoke with passion. They raised, and continue to raise, awareness on the campus and in the community. There were a number of players engaged in this process, but none more than Daelin Hayes, a defensive-end from Belleville, MI. He organized a Juneteenth rally and walk on campus in only a week. Hundreds of people attended and listened as Daelin spoke, along with teammates Myron Tagovailoa-Amosa and Max Siegel, Coach Kelly, and university president, Fr. John Jenkins. It was a moving day. The team represented for the whole world what is a great about Notre Dame Football—the people.

In the immediate aftermath of George Floyd's death and the unrest that followed, statements were being released everywhere, by both public figures and private citizens from across the country about what was happening. Social media became a primary outlet for the leadership in communities to express their feelings immediately. In our insulated world, we saw college football coaches from across the land take to Instagram and Twitter to express their support for the Black Lives Matter movement and condemn what had happened in Minnesota. Personally, I had a visceral reaction to what I saw. I was disgusted. But, before I engaged in any interactions through social-media, I wanted to take just a little bit of time to reflect.

I had a couple of concerns about speaking right away. First off, I didn't quite know what I had to offer of value. It's easy to say, "Racism is unacceptable." That is not an earth-shattering statement, and no person is putting themselves out on a limb by making it. But, in reality, I didn't want to talk about something I had never experienced myself. I have never been subjected to discrimination and felt unqualified to make a statement about what it was like to be a minority in our country. I did not want to be disingenuous.

Second, I did not want it to look like I was simply saying something, because I was afraid of how it might affect recruiting. My personal feeling was there were some coaches who were simply following the momentum of the social media wave and protecting themselves. Lastly and most importantly, I did not want to speak in public, when I knew there were times in my career I did not fully understand the point of view of a minority player. Many of the young men that I have worked with over the years have faced obstacles due to systematic and overt racism and socio-economic inequalities. In that time, there were instances when I did not do a good enough job of understanding their experiences and where they came from.

As the national conversations continued, I paid close attention and began to understand better the concept of being an "ally." I wanted to show some self-awareness. My career has been filled with opportunities to which other people don't have access. I have faced some obstacles, but not the kind that minorities face in the workforce. I wanted to acknowledge that and also show support for the people in our society who are not treated with equality. In the end, the only thing I could say, both in public and in private, is that I cannot understand how it feels to be the target of racism. I will never understand. I can only hope to learn by listening, not allowing racism to exist around me, and pledging to be part of the solution.

In thinking and talking about all of these dynamics and issues, the first thing that has become clear is that our society is at crossroads. Everyone has a choice to make right now. We can either: acknowledge that the life experiences of minorities in our country are different and in many cases, much more difficult, or choose to deny it. Apathy is not an option at this point. Any coach who ignores the fact that issues of race and inclusion are inherently important is hurting themselves in the eyes of their players.

Through all the different conversations, something became very clear to me. Coaches at the highest levels of sports, like football and basketball, where the majority of the players are African-American, can lose their perspective on the dynamics of race.

There are two issues at play. First, many coaches believe that racism is not as decisive an issue in a locker room, as it is in our society in general. There can be *some* truth to that; the teams I have been a part of are some of the most inclusive atmospheres I have ever encountered. However, for a coach to frame his experience with racism in the larger world, based on what he has observed inside a locker room is irresponsible. The two experiences simply do not equate.

Second, many coaches believe that because athletics are so performance-driven, issues of race and diversity are not a problem within a team culture. We have heard coaches at all levels talk, mistakenly, about how sports are the ultimate meritocracy and people are judged solely by their performance. This is simply not true. To think that race and diversity issues do not present themselves inside the framework of a team is unrealistic.

Any coach who says the words, "I don't see color," is taking the easy way out. What they are really saying is, "This conversation makes me uncomfortable, and I don't want to have it." To ignore race or cultural differences as a dynamic in a player/coach relationship is simply wrong. As coaches, we are kidding ourselves, if we think that it won't affect the dynamic at some point. It will affect it either positively or negatively, depending on how open we can be to accepting people for who they are and where they come from.

Failing to recognize a person's race is a failure to recognize that person as an individual. It is a refusal to see a person for who they are. If we cannot see a person as an individual, it is impossible to build a relationship with that person. We need to "see color," as well as other differences. By doing so, we are recognizing a person as unique, with a unique story and journey, all their own. By recognizing what makes a person unique, we are showing them they are valued. Acknowledging what makes people different is not a mistake. The mistake occurs when they are not viewed or treated as equals, based on those differences.

❑ Trying to Find Understanding

With all of the players and coaches I spoke to, one theme kept coming up repeatedly, *understanding.* We work with young, African-American men, many of whom feel like most coaches do not have enough understanding of where they come from and what challenges they face. In some cases, they feel like the coaches don't even want to make the effort to learn.

Our job is to show that we care about every single player, while still acknowledging that their life experiences can be different from our own. The *only* way to make that happen is through communication. We have to be willing to talk with one another, ask questions, and touch on uncomfortable topics if we are going to grow.

As growth occurs, trust begins to develop. Both the player and the coach understand that everyone is different and brings a different set of experiences and point of view into the relationship. That development allows all of us to accept people for who they are and then have compassion for one another.

Failing to recognize a person's race is a failure to recognize that person as an individual. It is a refusal to see a person for who they are.

Don Jackson spoke at length about this. Don was a three-year starter at running back at Nevada, a former captain, and a professional football player in the NFL and CFL. He was born and raised in Sacramento, CA and witnessed first-hand racism, drug culture in neighborhoods, and violence growing up. Don emphasized how important it is that a coach knows where a player comes from and have some sense of what that young man has experienced. The only way to do that is to take an interest and find out.

In the recruiting process, we have to keep our eyes open and talk *with* the prospect, and not *at* him. We need to ask questions and try to gain an honest appreciation for the unique challenges that each young person is facing. Then, we have to listen. Multiple players I spoke with mentioned that having someone simply listen to what they were dealing with was a great show of support. After we listen, we should validate what a player chooses to share with us; we cannot deny someone else's experiences. Nor, can we judge them based on those experiences either. It would have been completely wrong of me to draw conclusions about who Don Jackson is as a person, simply because he came from a bad neighborhood. However, having some understanding of where he comes from and what his life experiences have been helps me to find the best ways to connect with him as an individual.

I mentioned earlier that a number of young people in our country today are growing up in single-parent homes. This specifically affects our minority student-athletes. According to the US Census Bureau, in 2016, only 38 percent of African-American children lived in a two-parent home, compared to 74 percent of White children. I think that it is imperative that a coach know if a player did not have his father or another strong, male role model in his life growing up. This goes directly back to knowing and understanding the backgrounds of our young people.

One former player, an African-American, described how difficult the adjustment was going from his single-mother raising him to a world where all of the authority figures were men, and most were white. Honestly, I had never considered how different that might be. He talked at length about how we need to consider that some players have never had a man in their life before who has shown any interest in them, some have had men who model the wrong behaviors, and some have a natural distrust for men because of a negative experience. If we know these things about a player, then we can learn how better to approach him and adjust our style of teaching in hopes of building a healthier relationship.

There was one young man from my time at Nevada, with whom my inability to consider where he came from and his life's experience hurt our relationship. Ahki Muhammad was a defensive back who came from a crime-ridden, violent neighborhood in northern California. His mother raised him on her own, and you would describe his relationship with his father as difficult, at best.

Ahki did not have very many men in his life, certainly few white men, and he didn't trust them. He was an overachiever on the field. An underdog most of his life, because he was on the small side, he carried a chip on his shoulder that allowed him to compete at a higher level than he probably should have. In fact, it was what I loved about him. When it was going well, he was a joy. He was a bundle of energy, quick to smile, and had a great sense of humor. When it was not going well or someone challenged him, Ahki was quick to anger and was not afraid to fight in order to resolve a conflict. If an issue needing addressing or a matter of discipline came up, we always bristled against one another. That was my fault.

I failed to take into account that Ahki's experiences were different from mine. He did not have an inherent trust in the "coach," and he certainly did not like being called out by one in front of his peers. It was my job to understand that better. It was my job to put in the time with him, one-on-one, to earn his trust. It was also my job to be more patient with him.

I'm not saying Ahki didn't make mistakes that needed to be addressed; he made a handful. Rather, I'm saying that I made some difficult situations worse because of my lack of understanding. Looking back on our relationship, I know that I could have served Ahki better in some of those moments. I have since connected with him, and we had a very meaningful and honest conversation. I am very happy to say that our relationship is in a good place. I am also extremely proud of Ahki, as he is currently counseling at-risk youth in Oakland.

Having an understanding of where their players come from and what they have experienced is important for another reason as well. It can help guide us when making difficult decisions in regards to team standards and discipline. It is important to know that coaches have to know the players are watching when the staff disciplines a teammate. They are looking to see that each individual on the team, whether black or white, is treated fairly and consistently within the process. If they are not, the players recognize it, and it will become a problem in the locker room.

On the rare occasion when a player's violation of the rules merits considering suspension or non-renewal of his scholarship, it is important to remember how dramatic those consequences can be, and if they are more punitive than educational. Alabama head coach, Nick Saban, addressed this very thing a couple of years ago, when he was criticized for how he chose to handle the discipline of a player. The following are his thoughts: "There's always a lot of criticism out there when somebody does something wrong, everybody wants to know how you're going to punish the guy. But, there's not enough support for 19- and 20-year-old kids, people are out there saying, "Why do you give them another chance? Where do you want them to be? You want them to be in the street or do you want them to be here, graduating?"

I understand Coach Saban's perspective. There are too many people on the outside, who have no idea where a young person is from or what they might have experienced growing up, who want coaches to drop the hammer with the most severe punishment, when a student-athlete makes a mistake. We all acknowledge there are transgressions that require that type of reaction, but there are also times when a second chance is worth

One of the mistakes that I made earlier in my career was not a lack of understanding where a player had come from, but rather underestimating how dramatic the transition to a new environment could be.

giving. If we have a true understanding of a person's background, we might consider more carefully, when we chose to give those second chances and help young people to grow and learn, instead of taking away what might be their best chance to succeed in life.

❑ Support Through Transitions

The transition from high school to college is difficult for any young person. That said, research has shown that those who come from lower socioeconomic backgrounds are at a disadvantage when they go through it. Players, black and white, who come from poorer school districts and families that financially struggle, do not have access to the resources to help prepare them for the jump. In order to keep building strong relationships past recruiting, we have to be a source of support through that transition.

One of the mistakes that I made earlier in my career was not a lack of understanding where a player had come from, but rather underestimating how dramatic the transition to a new environment could be. I used to consider a recruit arriving on campus and think, "What could anyone complain about? This place is beautiful, and we are giving these guys everything they might need." That logic was flawed.

One former player described his transition to a college campus as "like moving to a foreign country." As odd as it sounded to me, he had never been around so many white people in his life. Dropped into a completely different culture, he expressed concern over how other students viewed him. Conversely, I have heard prospects and their parents celebrate the diversity of the LSU campus. One family commented they had never been in a university community that had as many people that "looked like we do."

This same topic comes up a lot on other campuses across the country, when you talk to the minority student-athletes. "You must play a sport?" is a question they hear often. Others on campus see them monolithically, only as athletes. The people around them make them feel as though their only path to a college education is through athletics. Football and basketball players in particular feel this, because often they are the biggest people in the room and stick out.

Another failure coaches make when thinking about a minority student-athlete's transition is the idea that a college campus is some sort of oasis that is immune from the problems that plague our society. It is just naïve to think that racism and bigotry will not rear their ugly heads at an institution of higher learning. Unfortunately, ugly reminders of this fact would appear year after year. We listened as players describe being pulled over for what they call "DWB" or "driving while black." We witnessed minority students treated differently by administrators and professors. We even saw two black players forced to finish a class remotely because a white student said she did not feel "safe" with them sitting in the room.

One particular event opened my eyes completely to what minority student-athletes can be forced to deal with. On September 24, 2016, our Nevada team traveled to play Purdue in West Lafayette, IN. It was a nationally televised game, appearing on the ESPN family of networks.

The timing is important, because earlier that fall, Colin Kaepernick, the quarterback for the San Francisco 49ers, had begun silently protesting police violence against minorities by kneeling during the national anthem. This started a national debate that was even more polarizing for our team and community, because Colin was a former player and graduate of Nevada.

Normally, our team was not on the field for the anthem so I never had to consider if they might protest. However, at Purdue, both squads were going to be on the field, while the song was played. In the days leading up to the game, there was some concern expressed to me by administrators that our players were going to join the protest. Let me be clear, no one ever came out and told me to not allow it. However, it was obvious that people were nervous about possible fallout, and they wanted me to address it with the team.

Personally, there was not much I was going to say. I, nor anyone else, could take away a person's freedom of expression. I just wanted to make sure that our team was respectful and that the players had talked about it collectively. In truth, I never knew if they were going to express themselves or not. During the anthem, a handful of players held fists in the air as show of solidarity for Colin and the cause. Television and photos captured the gesture. In the days that followed, the emails and voice messages I received were horrifying. What the players shared with me was even more so. That episode was an ugly reminder for me that there was really no place that was safe from racism and bigotry.

Recognizing that transitions are difficult is a first step, but we need to be able to provide consistent support, when our student-athletes arrive on campus. Again, if we are going to be dedicated to building healthy relationships with them, we have to be present and intent listeners, as they go through moments of adversity. No player expects his coaches to have all the answers, but they do expect that we will be there for them in difficult times to simply hear them and acknowledge what they are going through.

❑ Building Community

When we recruit a player and bring them onto a college campus, we are pulling them away from a community that they know well and understand. They are leaving their comfort zone. We have to help them build another comfort zone, away from their home. It is our responsibility to welcome them into and teach them about our communities. This is so important! We have to provide support by clearly explaining what the standards are.

Our goal is to make sure that everyone knows and is ready to adjust to the expectations that come along with being a member. This adjustment is about much more than just the training rules that exist in the football building. It is about teaching life on campus—conflict resolution, communication skills, relationship-building with professors and support staff, and developing bonds with peers in the residence halls and in classrooms. Players come to college, knowing they are going to receive high-level instruction on the field. We have to invest in them off the field and on campus, as well, so that we can set them up for success in the long term.

Mentorship is a valuable tool in helping young people adjust to the transition of joining a new community. By assigning players an "older brother" on the team who can guide them and answer questions, we are providing them another resource they can utilize. In the process, we are also showing trust in and giving ownership to the older players, as well. By telling the veterans, "His success is your success, and his difficulties are your difficulties," we are asking them to invest in their younger teammates. Those relationships create a culture of service, because players remember how important that mentorship was to them, and they want to provide it to a young player in the future.

Ryan Harris, a former player at Notre Dame, and a valued friend, told me a powerful story about the importance of community. Ryan is originally from Minneapolis, Minnesota and was recruited to the Irish by former head coach, Tyrone Willingham. Ryan is also a devout Muslim who dedicated himself to his religion at 14 years of age.

Even as one of the top high school players in the country, no other school he visited thought to bring him to a mosque, except for Notre Dame. Ryan described how impactful that was. Tyrone and the staff wanted to show that they had some understanding of the community he was coming from. They also wanted to assure him that his faith was welcome in the community they wanted him to join.

Shortly after Ryan began his career, Notre Dame ended their relationship with Coach Willingham and hired Charlie Weis to lead the program. This led to a second interaction that had a positive impact on Ryan. Coach Weis invited him to his office to talk and asked him a number of genuinely curious questions about his faith. Charlie wanted to learn more about Ryan's religious community and then wanted to celebrate the uniqueness of his journey. Coach Weis reached out to the sports information office and asked them to help tell Ryan's story to the public. Ryan spoke passionately about how meaningful those two connections were with his coaches, and they are great examples of building community.

❑ Being Mindful of Words

If we, as coaches, want to make sure that every player understands we value the relationship that we have with them, we must be mindful of the words that we choose. A good place to start when considering how we choose our words is to understand the term *microaggression*. The Merriam-Webster dictionary defines a microaggression as *a comment or action that subtly and often unconsciously or unintentionally expresses a prejudiced attitude toward a member of a marginalized group (such as a racial minority).* As one former player told me, "Microaggressions are real, and minority players have been recognizing them for years."

Microaggressions can come in the form of direct insults, in generalized opinions about a certain group of people, and by negating the feelings or experiences of others. Some are blatant and easy to pick out. A player once described to me a conversation where a female told him, "You're not like the other black guys I know from home; you are a good guy." Some are subtle and not so easy to identify, like offering a minority the compliment of being "articulate," as though we are surprised that a person of a particular race is able to expresses themselves well. Some, honestly, can be unintentional, like automatically assuming a person of Asian descent was born outside of the U.S.

No matter what form they come in, microaggressions do damage. They force the person on the receiving end to take calculated steps in deciding how they are going to respond. That person has to decide if it is worth their energy to explain to you why what you said was hurtful. Then, they have to deal with your reaction. Can you imagine going through your day, constantly worrying about how to deal with people who are treating you with disrespect? One person described it to me as "exhausting."

It feels like some of us are just starting to pay attention to the power that our words have on other people. And again, we are in a place where we have to decide how we are going to move forward. Either we can acknowledge the words we choose can sometimes affect other people negatively and try to do better, or we can simply choose to not care. What we cannot say is, "Hey, it's your problem that you feel this way." We cannot make it the fault of the other person.

Not only do we need to be mindful of those words that we choose as coaches, we also need to hold the players accountable as well. We have to ask them to be cognizant of the microaggressions they use against each other, but also against other genders and sexual orientations. We cannot allow the use homophobic or misogynistic language. It is never acceptable for a coach or a player to call someone a "bitch" or a "fag." If we are looking to create a culture of inclusiveness, we need to do it for everyone, across the board.

I once asked a player, if what is in a person's heart matters? After all, we are all human beings and are, by nature, flawed. "Yes," he answered, "What is in a person's heart matters. But, so do words, and people need to understand *intent versus impact* is real, and they don't always match."

Microaggressions often stem from unconscious biases. Sometimes, we are not even aware that we attributing specific stereotypes to different groups of people. Black players make "athletic" plays, and white players make "smart" plays. Being mindful of the words we choose is a positive step, but it can also be just surface-level thinking. We have to be willing to examine our beliefs deeply and honestly, because we can sometimes be unaware of them. Committing to rooting out biases is real work and is a necessary step in order to stop microaggressions and gain an understanding of other people. We have to adjust our beliefs before we can adjust our actions.

If we, as coaches, want to make sure that every player understands we value the relationship that we have with them, we must be mindful of the words that we choose.

❑ Accepting Cultural Differences

As long as there have been old coaches and young players, there has been a disconnect between cultures and choices. My dad would complain about my music, when I was a kid. He didn't understand it and didn't like it. I had baseball coaches who expected me to wear my uniform in a certain way; they did want my pant legs all the way down to my shoe tops. Those things are harmless. But, I have also known a coach who forced players to cut their hair, if it was hanging out the bottom of their helmets. That would be a problem for a player who was Rastafarian, whose dreadlocks held spiritual meaning for him.

This very scenario gained national attention in December of 2018, when a New Jersey referee told an African-American high school wrestler he would have to forfeit his match, unless he cut his dreadlocks. The young man had the trainer come out onto the mat and cut his hair right there on the spot. A year later, New Jersey lawmakers passed a bill making it illegal to discriminate, based on hairstyles associated with race.

Certain people will use the term "old school," as a way to explain why some of these expectations exist. Others will cite wanting everyone to look the same, symbolizing team over individual, as a reason. We have to be careful, because expectations like these things can lead coaches down a slippery slope. Unity does not mean uniformity. It is possible for a group of people to believe a common mission and set of values, without all looking the same. *Unique* and *united* are not mutually exclusive!

Building a real relationship with players means accepting them for who they are and allowing them, within the standards of the team, to express themselves. I am not advocating for removing all the rules. But, at some point, we cannot stifle every ounce of a young person's individuality. If the culture of our program is accountability, toughness, and effort, then, I am going to judge a player based on his knowledge of his assignments, his physicality, and his energy. I am not going to judge him based on his hair or how he wears his socks. Within the standards of the program, we have to be willing to let people have some uniqueness.

More importantly, we cannot judge or be afraid of an individual, simply because what makes him unique derives from a culture of which we are not familiar. At Nevada, I had an issue with two players wearing gold teeth in pre-game warm-ups. The fact they were wearing those teeth had no effect on how they did their jobs and played the game. In fact, both men embodied the standards that we set for the program. The issue was mine; I was just uncomfortable with the image of gold teeth and had to get over it.

Something in my subconscious just associated gold teeth with bad dudes. I was wrong. I learned that we have to stop using the associations we developed through the culture we grew up in to judge the choices of people who grew up in a culture that was completely different. It is also important to remember that is not our job to get a player to conform to what we think society will deem acceptable. The world has always been a diverse place; you can be an exceptional person and have gold teeth, earrings, tattoos, and long hair. If a player is living up to the standards of the program, on and off the field, it is not our place to tell him how to dress, how to wear his hair, or what music to enjoy.

❑ Moving Forward

I asked every person to whom I spoke about this topic what is the most important thing that a non-minority coach can do to build stronger relationships with minority student-athletes. The answer was always a version of the same thought; we need to have open doors and have open dialogue. By making a point of consistently checking in with and being available for, we are showing minority players support.

Ryan Harris spoke about doing more to prepare our minority student-athletes for life after sports and providing them with the tools to be successful off the field. He mentioned specifically the need to teach financial literacy to players, before they leave school. He shared stories about peers in the NFL who did not take care of their money and how their lives could have been different, if someone had taken the time to help prepare them for the choices they were going to make.

This factor has become even more important now in the day and age of name, image, and likeness. The NCAA, and some high school associations, are now allowing

fizkes/Shutterstock.com

What is the most important thing that a non-minority coach can do to build stronger relationships with minority student-athletes—have open doors and have open dialogue.

student-athletes to benefit financially through endorsements and other available avenues. A lot of young men and women across the country are coming into money that they are not used to having and need guidance learning how to manage it responsibly.

Asauni Rufus, a former captain at Nevada and currently an assistant coach for the San Francisco 49ers, spoke at length about helping young men develop character and leaderships skills. Then, when those men who come from difficult places go back to their communities, they can be positive male role models. They can use the skills they have learned to break the negative cycles and lead the change.

Daelin Hayes and Sean Crawford, former players at Notre Dame, both talked about their desire to have an African-American male on the football staff, in a non-coaching role. They felt like having someone in the building every day, who could relate to the experiences of black players and offer wisdom and guidance, would be an incredibly valuable asset and help players transition more smoothly.

Their thoughts led me to think more about minority representation on coaching staffs. As an administrator, I will dedicate myself moving forward to providing young minority coaches with opportunities in entry-level jobs. I want to look for minority candidates who just need a chance to break in at a high level. I also want to be a better mentor and share my knowledge in order to help prepare them to succeed as they move up in the profession.

As coaches, we tell players all the time that in order to achieve any meaningful growth, they have to learn how to leave their comfort zones. The opportunity to speak with all of these different people about the topics of race and inclusion was my opportunity to leave my comfort zone and to learn. It is not easy to hear someone you care about tell you that you could have done better. It is also not easy to look back and recognize where your thinking or your approach was flawed. While it is not easy, and it is not comfortable, it is certainly necessary. The whole point of this project is to help coaches and teachers build healthier relationships with student-athletes, so that they can serve them better. In order to do that, we have to be willing to listen. I am grateful for the courage and the honesty that it took for some of these young men to share what they did. Moving ahead in my career, I know that I am better off for it.

CHAPTER 7

Who Is Generation Z?

Generation Z is an incredibly unique group of people. They are coming of age during a tumultuous period in our world's history, their ethnic backgrounds are the most diverse the United States has ever seen, and they have been raised and educated in homes and schools that would have been considered non-traditional by the generations coming before them. For parents, teachers, coaches, and supervisors to better understand Generation Z, we must know who they are, the world that they have grown up in and have been shaped by, and what specifically makes them different from previous groups of young people. If we know who they are, we have a much better chance of developing connections and building meaningful relationships with them.

❑ Makeup of Generation Z

Generation Z is made up of young Americans born between the years of 1995 and 2010 and consists of approximately 70 million people—roughly 25 percent of the U.S. population. It is the most ethnically diverse generation in the history of our country. Approximately 50 percent are white (non-Hispanic), 25 percent are Hispanic, 14 percent are Black, 6 percent are Asian, and 5 percent are either of mixed race or another ethnicity. This is the first generation in the U.S. that is not majority white. That is a stunning statistic and offers some insight into Generation Z's expectations about diversity. They have grown up in a world, where they are used to seeing people who do not all look the same.

❑ Socio-Economics

This generation will produce more children from a single-parent home than from any group before it. 36 percent of Generation Z will be born to unwed mothers, up from 25 percent for Millennials. In their lifetime, they will have lived in 10+ homes and worked 12+ different jobs, on average. Upon retirement, the average salary will be just under $250,000.

❑ Education

Members of Generation Z are more likely to be raised in a household where at least one parent has a bachelor's degree. That said, only 50 percent will attend college, as Generation Z will embrace non-traditional ways of learning and gaining expertise. They will spend less time on homework, extracurricular activities, and volunteering. Employers are being forced to adjust. More and more people are being hired for a specific skill set and trained on the job. The "business," in some ways, is becoming the "university," with employers understanding that education has to continue in the workplace.

❑ Social/Cultural

Fewer and fewer young people in Generation Z will be raised in religiously affiliated homes. While a number will describe themselves as "spiritual," in nature, less will associate themselves with a specific religion.

Regarding drugs and alcohol, they view the use of marijuana as safer than the use of alcohol. Just 40 percent will drink in high school, which signifies a significant shift in attitudes from Millennials, who grew up in era where marijuana was vilified in mainstream culture.

Sexual identification and sexual activity have also changed a great deal with this group. Less than 80 percent of Generation Z will identify themselves as "straight" or "heterosexual." 12 percent identify themselves as bisexual, which is more than double that of Millennials. While more open to identifying themselves and others outside of the norms, sexual activity for Generation Z has decreased. More Gen Zers between the ages of 18-24 are reporting no sexual partners than both Millennials and Gen Xers.

The world in which Generation Z is coming of age is a much different place than the one in which Millennials and Generation X grew up. Advances in technology have made access to information easier than it has ever been before and has changed that way people live their daily lives. On the other hand, a pandemic, economic strife, terrorism, and global conflict have created an atmosphere of anxiety for young people. It is important that we understand the events that have shaped Generation Z.

❑ Technology

In the world of Gen Zers, technology is permanently on and constantly accessible. Generation Z will average over 10 hours a day, utilizing technology, over five different screens. They will draw their social cues from technology—they learn how to act from what they watch and interact with over screens. Nearly 50 percent of Gen Zers admit that what they read/see on social media affects how they feel about themselves.

❑ Terrorism

Young people today have grown up in a post 9/11 world. Their entire lives they have had to take off their shoes and go through a metal detector at the airport. They have seen armed guards in public view. They have turned on the TV to see bombs exploding busses and buildings across the world.

❑ Global Recession

Most Gen Zers have come of age during financial crises of 2005 and 2008. They have witnessed parents and family members losing jobs, retirement funds, and homes. 79 percent of Generation Z reports that they are concerned about finding a good job that will enable them to provide, and they are willing to sacrifice fulfillment for financial security.

❑ Pandemic

The data on the effects of Coronavirus and the pandemic are incomplete and will be for quite some time. What we do know thus far is that it affected people's mental health greatly, including Gen Zers. It left them with a heightened sense of anxiety and feeling isolated. It affected such things as social development, education, and the ability to function in the workplace, to name a few. In several cases, the pandemic was the first experience of true adversity and became a catalyst for the development of resilience.

We have touched on the make-up of Generation Z, who they are, and the events and movements in their lifetime that have shaped them. However, the most important step is understanding the things that make them so different from their predecessors. Without this knowledge, it's nearly impossible to work with them effectively.

❑ Relationship-Driven

Relationships come first. If Gen Zers are going to produce to their highest capabilities, whether it be on the field, in the classroom, or at work, it is because they feel connected to the people that they are working for and alongside of. They want to know that we are interested in them, that we care, and that we want to see them succeed. Their respect and trust must be earned. They have access to all the information that they could possibly want, it is the connections with coaches, teachers, and peers that make the experience worthwhile.

❑ Instantaneous Thinkers

The brain of a Generation Z young person has evolved to process information faster. In the history of mankind, the speed and access to information is at all-time high, and they have adjusted to handle it. As a result, they lose interest more quickly, as well. The average attention span is now between six-to-eight seconds, down from 12 seconds in 2000. Even communication has become faster, as emoji's have replaced words or complete sentences.

❑ Independent Learners

Because Gen Zers have grown up in the digital age, they have discovered a world of information at their fingertips. In the past, in order to learn something, young people had to find a parent, teacher, or coach who could instruct them and help them develop a particular talent or interest. That is no longer the case.

Today, learning to play guitar is as simple as a Google search on a laptop. Identifying and practicing the fundamentals of shooting a free-throw in basketball can be found on YouTube. My niece, Caroline, is in the summer between her junior and senior years in high school and is taking a creative writing class from University of North Carolina that is being taught online. She worked from a hot-spot and a laptop during a seven-hour car ride and knocked out three classes. That would have been impossible twenty years ago. If Generation Z wants to learn something, they can do so from a variety of different outlets and on their own timeline.

❑ Anxiety

Members of Generation Z are growing up in a time of increased stress, depression, and anxiety. Some 70 percent of teenagers today, across all gender, race, and socioeconomic strata, report that mental health is a problem among their peers. Technology plays a role in this, as they are exposed to an endless stream of negative news stories and struggle in living up to the "social-media" worthy lives of other people.

We hear the term "negative affect" used to describe this group often. They are generally a pessimistic bunch and tend to look at life through a negative lens. This is the first generation in decades that feels like their lives are going to be more difficult than that of their parents.

They also harbor fear of what the future might hold for them. The pandemic was a scarring event. They fear military conflict and acts of terrorism. They fear growing debt and financial insecurity. Their fear is real and can be debilitating.

❑ Loneliness

This characteristic defies some general logic, as Gen Zers are the most technologically connected group in history. They can talk, text, or direct message instantaneously. Even in a time of social networking, when it has never been easier to make new "friends," they still describe themselves as being lonely. Generation Z is craving interpersonal interaction and connection with other people.

❑ Authenticity

As was mentioned earlier, Gen Z has grown up during a turbulent time in history. That experience has allowed them to recognize the difference between the illusion of a "perfect world" and the harsh reality of real life. As digital natives, they have experience with marketers and peers trying to hide every imperfection. They are not easily fooled.

Young people today are truer to themselves than any group before. They do not want to be viewed as a pretender and do not want to associate themselves with people who are viewed as pretenders. They seek relationships with people who are going to "keep it real"—people who are going to be honest and consistent with them.

Authenticity can also manifest itself in humor, and Generation Z's sense of humor is outlandish and creative. They have a unique ability to use social media and meme culture to identify current trends and then make light of them, almost overnight. They can be ironic, self-deprecating, and sometimes, just plain weird.

❑ Risk Averse

Because of the instability the Generation Z has experienced in their lifetime, they are generally risk averse. That term does not speak only to their financial approach, but also to the way they go about their everyday lives. They are looking for safety and stability. They are looking for practicality. Statistics show that Gen Z drivers are significantly safer than the Millennials who came before them. They are getting fewer moving violations, getting in fewer accidents, and being cited for less DWIs. One expert described Generation Z as being "the physically safest generation, but yet the most mentally and emotionally fragile."

afotostock/Shutterstock.com

Young people today seek relationships with people who are going to "keep it real"—people who are going to be honest and consistent with them.

❑ Late to Develop Resilience

There was a school of thought for a long period of time that young people today lacked resilience, or the ability to display grittiness through adversity. Part of that thinking was centered around the concept of "snow-plow" parenting; that most parents today would clear all the challenges out of the way for their children, and as a result, their kids would have little experience dealing with adversity. In some ways, that was true. However, most experts believe that the COVID pandemic proved to be a seminal moment for Generation Z and has allowed them to develop and use a new-found resiliency.

There was no "clearing out" the challenges that the pandemic presented. Young people were forced to face illness, loss of loved ones, isolation, job/financial insecurities, and shifts in education. Most Gen Zers grew from the experience and developed some of the grit that so many thought they lacked. We will dive into to that further a little later.

When we study each generation individually, we identify things, traits, and markers that make each of them unique. Generations take shape in different periods of time and are formed and influenced, in part, by the world around them. However, with Generation Z, there are distinct qualities and characteristics that make them very different from all the others and have forced teachers, coaches, and administrators to adjust. Because of these distinctions, engaging and connecting with them has become more difficult. With understanding of what makes them unique comes a better and more intentional plan for building relationships with them.

CHAPTER 8

Connecting With Generation Z

If you are in teaching, coaching, or in any leadership role for a long enough, you will be forced to adjust to the different generations with whom you are working. Trying to effectively communicate and build relationships with young people, who are vastly different than the groups that came before them, is one of the great challenges of the job. Working with Generation Z presents interesting obstacles, but also some exciting opportunities.

When dealing with Generation Z, you have to let go of your preconceived notions. The way that you learned and felt most comfortable communicating as a young adult is NOT the way this generation is going to learn and communicate. In order to achieve your goals of relating to them, you must assume the responsibility of changing. You must find the best ways to reach your audience. It is your job to adjust to them, not their job to adjust to you.

In the last couple of years, I have tried to learn more about how Generation Z learns, how they communicate, and how better to connect and build relationships with them. Some of the knowledge gained and the tools used were discovered through other people's research and data. Some was formed through personal experience and through trial and error. The following are some thoughts that might help you work more efficiently and effectively with this generation:

❑ Generation Z Is Independent

Gen Z is more self-directed and independent than previous generations. They also have a positive self-image. They have been told that they can take on the world—coaches should encourage that—in both success and failure.

What this group has gained in independence, they sometimes lack in real-life wisdom or what some might consider "street-smarts." You have to protect them in some parts of their lives from this. They can be taken advantage in ways such as cyber-bullying, catfishing, or simply being scammed by people older than themselves. Their independence comes along with an innocence, as well.

❑ Generation Z Craves Interpersonal Interaction

Through the course of history, communication has never been faster or easier than it currently is. That does not mean that Gen Z doesn't crave "face-to-face" interaction. They do. If given the choice between a phone call or text and a face-to-face conversation, this generation still wants the intimacy of being in the presence of the other person. However, one shift in regards to technology and communication is that they consider simply "seeing" you as face to face. A Zoom meeting or a Facetime call is viewed the same as sitting across from you in a room.

They enjoy conversations—but they want to be talked *with*, not talked *to*. The give and take that comes with two people talking with one another helps strengthen their relationships.

❑ Generation Z Wants to Engage and Have a Voice

Generation Z is the most informed and savvy generation in history. Social media has provided them with a platform to express themselves on serious topics, sometimes, even before they are old enough to vote. Think about the social impact a group of high school students had in the wake of the Parkland shootings in Florida. They were able to draw national attention and start a conversation about gun laws in our country.

They have learned critical-thinking skills and have engaged in a level of debate that previous generations have not. They are less concerned about typical "teenage" concerns and are thinking about sophisticated issues. Coaches and teachers must not take their desire to have a voice for granted and also should not underestimate how engaged and educated they will be about the issues.

When dealing with Generation Z, you have to let go of your preconceived notions.

❑ Generation Z Expects You to Listen

Generation Z has grown up with parents listening to them, and in some cases, hanging on their every word. They expect that when they communicate with you, that you are going to listen. They also know when they are being ignored, which can be a major obstacle in building relationships.

Coaches have to make a point of listening to their players, and the really savvy ones know when to let the players have a voice. If the head coach allows the players to voice an opinion on a decision that he doesn't see as critical in the big picture, it buys him credibility with the team. For example, changing the menu at a team meal. To the players, that might be a big deal. To the head coach, it may not be as important. In that situation, it's a good investment by the coach to give the players what they ask for. Then, later on, when a decision comes up that the head coach feels strongly about, the players are more likely to follow his lead, because they know they have been heard in the past.

❑ Generation Z Will Compete

Sports have been woven into the fabric of the lives of the members of Generation Z. The NFL, the NBA, and NCAA athletics have all hit all-time highs in terms of engagement and exposure in the lifetime of Gen Zers. The concept of winning and losing is not the least bit foreign to them. Competition for them has not been exclusive to just athletics either. These kids have been judged against one another for most of their lives in such things as science, math, debate, and dance, to name just a few. Coaches should not be afraid to challenge this generation to compete.

❑ Learning Environment

Structure in the classroom, in the meeting room, and on the field is a must. Generation Z has a shorter attention span than those who came before them. We have to be efficient with the time, when Gen Zers are focused. By presenting an agenda for the day, setting goals, and providing challenges, we help them to be more organized and productive learners. When players came into my special teams meeting, the title slide on the screen would show them what units were working, what was being covered in the meeting, and what we were trying to achieve on the field with that day's script. Boring is bad! We always have to be showing them what's next.

As students and players, they want feedback, and they want it often. They have grown up in a world, where results are often available instantaneously. They can go online and check their grades, they can check their phones to see exactly how far they have run, and technology like Catapult can tell them exactly how fast they ran at practice that day. They are used to receiving feedback, both positive and negative, in regular intervals. Coaches and teachers must be able to provide it.

❑ Generation Z Wants to See the Big Picture

For most of their lives, the road to success has been laid out for Gen Zers. You cannot be afraid to show them the view from 30,000 feet and make sure they understand the "why" of what you are asking them to do. The days of saying, "Just do it because I told you to" are over. If you are willing to take a little extra time to explain why you are doing what you are doing, you are showing investment in them. That builds credibility.

Competency is also really important, if you want them to follow you. Gen Zers want to look up to you and to learn from you, but they will only do that if they truly believe that you know what you are talking about and you can make them better.

❑ Generation Z Desires Practical Skills

While it is important that young people understand the "big picture," they also want to learn practical skills that they can put to use. A coach or teacher must be able to teach the fundamentals that will directly affect their ability to succeed. What's more, they want customized teaching. You must provide what the individual needs, as opposed to the cookie-cutter presentation given the same way to each group.

Coaches who go out every single day and repeat the same drills over and over again are not going to optimize Gen Z. They want to focus their work on specifically what needs improving, and they want it personalized by player. They are willing to stay and do extra work, as long as the work is individualized.

❑ Generation Z Is Financially Focused

This generation watched their parents, their families, and their friends' families survive a great recession. Homes were foreclosed, jobs were lost, and a number of people were just trying to survive. This group is sensitive to that. When Generation Z thinks about their futures, they want fulfillment. On the other hand, they are also pragmatic, and they will not sacrifice financial stability in order to have it.

They also have an entrepreneurial spirit. Remember, this generation watched Mark Zuckerberg form Facebook and make a billion dollars, before he was 25 years old. The thought of creating something that big and successful is not a wild dream to them.

This factor really comes into play in recruiting. More and more young people are evaluating their college choices, according to what school might provide the best opportunity to earn a living after graduation. Graduation rates, specialized schools of study, and starting salaries are all factoring in. Keep in mind, for high school football players, playing in the NFL is also considered a way to earn a living. They are evaluating schools, based on who has developed players and helped prepare them for the next level. We are seeing more and more of this due to NIL. Recruited student-athletes are not always choosing the schools they always dreamed of going to; sometimes, they are choosing the programs that provide a pathway to providing for their families.

❑ Generation Z Is Creative

Generation Z is comfortable trying to be innovative. They have grown up seeing young people, just like them, start businesses, produce incredible art, and lead scientific discovery. This group is not afraid to try and find solutions, and you should let them try, because they can succeed in ways that you never thought possible.

❑ Generation Z Is Adaptable

Because Gen Zers have grown up with an incredible amount of knowledge, literally at their fingertips, they are not afraid to seek new information or ideas. The thought of trying something, failing at it, and then trying another way is completely comfortable to them. They can change direction with ease in a way that might make older generations panic.

If something is not working schematically, or there is a need to change in a specific week in order to increase the chances of success, Gen Z can handle it easily. This can be really valuable at the high school level, where the strengths and weaknesses of the personnel can dictate what style you have to play in any given year. They will adjust seamlessly.

❑ Peer Opinions Matter to Generation Z

The opinions of the peers of Gen Zers matter to this group of young people, just as much as those of their parents, teachers, or coaches. In a classroom, within a team, or inside a business setting, peer-accountability groups become incredibly valuable, because they are effective tools in helping develop and uphold standards.

Within the Notre Dame and LSU football programs, we had the S.W.A.T. program (Summer Workout Accountability Teams). The coaching staff selected the SWAT captains, who were often upper-classmen and are always a collection of players who embodied the values of the program. Those guys then drafted their teammates from across the roster and competed with the other teams throughout the course of the year. They were awarded points for such things as weight-room performance, academic performance, communication with staff, and community service. When guys weren't holding up their end of the bargain, it was their SWAT team leaders and teammates who addressed the issues.

❑ Generation Z Is All About Technology

Generation Z has grown up in a digital era. They have no memory of a house phone, with a tangled chord that's attached to a wall! The use of technology in the learning process in not only common, it's expected. You have to be willing to find ways to use technology in teaching. iPads, computers, film clips sent to phones—these are all tools that you must make use of in order to best engage them.

This group communicates freely and quickly through the use of technology, and you have to adjust. Email, text, or direct messaging in order to talk with someone is not considered the least bit unusual. There are some social cues that you have to adjust to, as well. Generation Z will seek out and appreciate face-to-face interaction, but does not value eye contact the way their parents did. The reason is simple; they have had a device in their hands for all of their lives. There is no sense that a lack of eye contact is a sign of disrespect, because they have grown used to talking with people, while looking down at their phones.

❑ Diversity Is the Expectation

Generation Z will be the first in American history that is not majority white. They are the most racially and ethnically diverse generation we have ever seen. In their lifetime, they have already witnessed the election of an African-American president and the legalization of gay marriage.

This group of young people acknowledges the racial inequality that exists in our country more easily than those before them. They are also more open to, and in a lot of cases, encouraging of social change in American society. Diversity is their normal and their expectation.

❑ Generation Z Wants to Have Fun

Young people want to enjoy their peers, their work place, and the challenges they face. They want to make friends in school, in the locker room, or at work. Coaches have to be creative in the ways they engage, motivate, and teach Gen Zers. We have to find ways to create fun, make them laugh, and keep them interacting with one another!

Generation Z is such a unique group. They were born in the digital age, yet they share a lot of old-school values from generations that came before them. FutureCast President Jeff Fromm characterized this demographic group as "old souls in young bodies." In some ways, they are aligned more with "Baby Boomers" than they are with "Millennials."

A number of the ways that we communicated with players from years past will still connect with this group. We can draw from their independence, their desire to compete, and their willingness to work on their skills. In other ways, they are dramatically different. We have to be willing to engage them in the conversation and listen to what they have to say. We must explain the "why" of what we are asking them to do. And we have to be willing to use technology as a teaching tool and an important vehicle for communication. Building relationships with Generation Z is incredibly important, if we want to serve them to the best of our ability. It can also be challenging and a whole lot of fun.

CHAPTER 9

Giving Generation Z Feedback

A lack of effective communication can lead to a breakdown in relationships, especially with Generation Z. It is essential that we study and rethink how we express ourselves and listen. Giving and receiving feedback is the most important tool for providing constructive information in the communication process. It is also instrumental in developing healthy relationships.

Dictionary.com defines feedback as *a reaction or a response given to a particular process or activity, and the evaluative information derived from such a reaction or response.* In athletics, we watch a player in practice or in a game, and then, we provide either positive or negative responses. In most cases, we provide both. That player then processes the information he has received and tries to learn something from it. In a classroom setting, a student writes a rough draft. The teacher points out where the paper is strong and where it needs bolstering. The student then goes back to work on the final version of the paper.

Feedback is important for a number of reasons, and it can have a positive impact on the person giving it, the person receiving it, and the relationship overall. One of the main reasons that it is so important is that feedback is *always* available. It is an endless source of information to glean and learn from.

Feedback is available in different forms. It's available in traditional, formal settings, like schools, sports teams, and businesses. As children, parent/teacher conferences and report cards provided feedback about academic performance. As athletes, the coaches provided us feedback about performance on the practice field, in the meeting room, and on the sidelines during a game. In adulthood, things like the comment section, surveys, and performance reviews serve as avenues for us to gather observations about our work.

There are also informal ways to gather feedback, and they occur every day, all around us. What is the body language of the people to whom I am speaking? Are they listening to me intently? What kind of feedback am I sending with my volume and tone? These are verbal and non-verbal clues that we send to one another in every interaction, and they are all versions of feedback.

In general terms, feedback opens the door for further and more detailed communication. When a person can utilize comfortable, direct, and respectful ways of giving feedback, it encourages others to do the same. It starts conversations.

When conversations begin, then the opportunity for growth occurs, on both sides. Relationships will strengthen with the use of feedback, because when it is given honestly and correctly, it helps people evolve.

Feedback also allows for people and organizations to avoid the catastrophic mistake. When information and observations are shared honestly and consistently, it is easier to keep everyone on the same page and pointed in the right direction. Feedback should eliminate errors caused by miscommunication, prevent you from having to correct the same mistake repeatedly, and make the organization more efficient.

For example, in my own experience, we wanted to make a dramatic change in punt protection at Notre Dame in 2007. For years, I had only used one style, but times were changing, and I felt like we needed to evolve. The head coach at the time, Charlie Weis, agreed but stayed very involved. We talked about what we were doing often, and he pointed out to me flaws in the scheme and in the techniques. Because there was consistent feedback, we identified where the problems might be and addressed them. That was far better than never communicating and having those flaws exposed by a blocked punt that could have cost us a game.

Working environments where people are open to constructive criticism, or better yet, places where people *seek* constructive criticism are often among industry leaders. Feedback spurs change and innovation. Environments like these are places where people get unstuck, and problems are solved. It is amazing how many times

Feedback opens the door for further and more detailed communication.

the solution to a problem is found, because someone felt comfortable enough to share an observation or a thought, and someone else was secure enough to hear it. An atmosphere where feedback is encouraged is an atmosphere that is going to be productive and successful.

In the opening chapter, I referenced the 2016 season for the Notre Dame football program. The Fighting Irish struggled to a 4-8 record, which is far below the lofty standards of a place that has been a national power for nearly a century. When a season goes that poorly at a place that is used to sustained success, serious reflection takes place by the people charged with overseeing the program. The president, Fr. John Jenkins, the athletic director, Jack Swarbrick, and the head coach, Brian Kelly, all got together and took stock of the program. Honest conversations occurred about what needed to take place in order to get the team back to healthy place. I am sure the feedback that was given at that meeting was not always easy to hear.

Moving forward, Coach Kelly met with the leadership of the team, as well as others around the program. He expressed his thoughts, both positive and negative, but was also humble enough to allow each of the people he met with to share their thoughts. In a terrific example of leadership, he gave important and actionable feedback, but also accepted it at the same time.

The result of those conversations were dramatic changes around the football operation. Incredibly difficult decisions were made around staffing. New procedures were put in place. Player-led leadership within the locker room was re-emphasized and re-organized. Coach Kelly himself, after years of high-level success doing it in a specific manner, adjusted some of the ways that he approached his job.

Some of these things occurred before I arrived, others after, to which I was personal witness. Either way, it served as an important learning experience for me as a coach. Feedback, given honestly and thoughtfully, led to the winningest five-year run in the history of Notre Dame football.

❑ Giving Feedback Is Important

Giving another person feedback is important for several reasons. First and foremost, when we provide it, we are showing that individual that they are significant to us! We have sacrificed our time to observe them and their work, we have carefully thought about the information we were going to share with them, and we have considered an action plan for them to get better. Giving feedback is an investment in someone else. It is a sign that person is important to you as an individual. If our people know that we care about them, they are more likely to care about us and work harder in order to try to improve. This is especially important to Generation Z, because they are so relationship-driven.

Another reason that providing feedback is important in a relationship is because it can serve as a source of motivation. We are trying to enable and encourage our student-athletes to be the best versions of themselves. We aid in that task by sharing with them not only what we think they do well, but also areas where we think they can improve. Our goal is to help them build self-esteem, while still serving as a force to help them keep moving forward. By providing clear guidance on how to improve and investing in that improvement, we are motivating people to get better and to boost their production.

There was an interesting psychological study done in 1951 by Donald O. Hebb at McGill University in Montreal. In his study, Hebb placed male graduate students in small chambers and observed them over the course of a few days. What he discovered was a person in isolation would quickly begin to suffer from depressive moods, paranoia, and even hallucinations. Their mental faculties become temporarily impaired. It is important to remember that most people *want* feedback. Accordingly, we need to be able to provide it. Human beings are relational—they want to interact with others.

Human beings need outside stimuli, and if they don't receive it, they can "go nuts." As it relates to feedback, the same rule applies. In a school or work setting, if we never provide any feedback, we leave our people wondering what we are thinking. They are left to try and figure out how they are doing by analyzing our every look, gesture, or word. It can create for a nerve-wracking experience.

In the same way that students in school and professionals at work want feedback, the overwhelming majority of the players we work with *want* to be coached as well. Athletes, in general, are driven to improve and seek out information that will help make them better. They want to know when they do it well, when they do it poorly, and what they can do to improve. As coaches, if we are not constantly providing that information and the steps to develop, we are not doing our jobs. Sharing feedback with our players should be our top priority. It's free to hand out, and it's easy. The only thing it requires from us is the willingness to evaluate our players and the desire to help them.

Being skilled at giving constructive feedback increases your own value as well. If you can give feedback that your people can hear, understand, and utilize, you are able to optimize them. Any assistant coach who gets the most out of his players is more valuable in the eyes of the head coach and the administration. Being known as a coach who will help his guys reach their full potential is a good reputation to have.

Also, it builds your credibility. When you are invested and thoughtful about these conversations, you gain the trust and the respect of the people with whom you are working. As a result, they are less likely to react defensively, when you offer a critical review. For every positive interaction that you have, you build up goodwill. That goodwill is currency. It can provide you the benefit of the doubt, if you say something that can be taken the wrong way. Coaches who care about providing feedback to their players, as well as care about the way it is given, earn the trust of their guys and are more effective teachers because of it. Gen Zers are going to make you earn their trust.

Finally, if you develop the skills to properly give feedback, people are going to want to hear what you have to say. When a critical moment arrives, and you need a message to be heard, the more likely the people around you are going to listen to and understand your message. Coaches who have built up credibility with their players can get them to stay calm and hear what is being said when things are moving fast. This factor is especially important, when things aren't going well.

❑ Receiving Feedback Is Important

Being able to accept the information that is shared with us is an important part of the growth process, both personally and professionally. It is recognition that no matter what stage of our career or life we are in, we can always learn something new and improve ourselves. The steps we take when receiving feedback are no different than the basic learning process for every human being. First, we must be intentional listeners. There is a reason they call it "paying attention"—we have to put forth the effort to focus on what is being said. Then, we must take the time to think about what we have heard and organize our response. Finally, we have to arrive at a solution and an action plan in order to affect the changes we are looking for. This process is the basis of growth.

The most elemental part of receiving feedback is being open to hearing it. Most people can handle hearing positive things about themselves, but a lot of people find it difficult to hear any criticism. Any version of feedback is most likely going to have some criticism. Hopefully, it is constructive criticism, but it will be criticism nonetheless.

It's hard to hear someone tell you that your work could be improved. Receiving feedback takes maturity and a sense of security or self-worth. Ego and pride have to be set aside, and the focus needs to remain on the goal, and the goal is always

Dmitry Demidovich/Shutterstock.com

Coaches who have built up credibility with their players can get them to stay calm and hear what is being said when things are moving fast.

to get better. When we are open to others' observations and suggestions, we are giving ourselves a chance to improve and grow in a number of different ways. This can be hard for some coaches, because most are "alpha" personalities and are used to delivering feedback, instead of receiving it. The best coaches though, like the best players, seek feedback and want to know where they can get better.

When we can learn to accept feedback comfortably, it allows us to feel a greater sense of belonging and purpose. It can be inspiring. Everyone wants to know that they are valued. When our head coach or a peer on the staff takes the time to offer constructive criticism or recognize our contributions, it is validating. It shows that other person is willing to invest in us, that they are interested in our development and future. That is a powerful feeling. It can drive us to achieve at even higher levels. We all want to feel like an important and contributing member of a winning team. In order to do that, we have to be open to accepting feedback.

Some people reach a point where they are no longer interested in growth. They either don't want to put the effort in to learn something new, or they feel like they have all the answers already. Others are always looking to get better. Eric Musselman is a great example of this. Eric, the head basketball coach at the University of Arkansas, has coached in the CBA, the D-League, and the NBA as well as in college.

Coach Musselman and I were at Nevada at the same time, and one winter, he invited me over to watch his team practice. I really enjoyed watching him and his staff, and the players work. I was totally into what was happening on the court and was taking some notes. When practice was over, Eric came over to where I was sitting on the bench and asked me what I thought. He knew full well that I was not a basketball expert but wanted to know if I saw anything they might be able to improve. I was blown away by the fact that he felt like he could possibly learn something from me. Here was a coach who was at the highest levels of his profession, and he was wondering what a fresh set of eyes might have seen at his practice. His humility and curiosity left a powerful and lasting impression.

If people can accept constructive criticism, it can have a positive effect on how others see them. Coaches who can handle feedback are viewed as unpretentious workers, who are open to improving every day. They are also seen as more approachable, and this can help in interactions with other coaches or members of the staff. Head coaches and administrators want to be around assistants who can handle feedback, because it makes them more comfortable around you, as well as makes their jobs easier. That, in turn, strengthens your relationships with your supervisors.

In the end, good coaches understand that high achievers want to know what they can do to get better; they are constantly seeking feedback, so that they can address any weaknesses, real or perceived. One of the strongest compliments a coach can give a player is to call him "coachable." We must be "coachable," as well. If we want to continue to grow and get better, we must be able to accept and learn from the feedback of others.

❑ Principles of Giving Feedback

Giving feedback is a skill and a vital part of a coach's job description. It is extremely important that when feedback is given, it is delivered the proper way. When it is done correctly, it can be a powerful tool. When done poorly, it can be damaging. Constructive criticism that is delivered without thoughtfulness or care can upset people, have a negative effect on their self-esteem, and make them feel under-appreciated. With young people today, it can also due damage to the connections we work so hard to build. None of those feelings lead to improved production or growth. The following are some tips to keep in mind for delivering feedback well with Generation Z:

- *Time and place.* Pick an appropriate time and place to share feedback. A private setting is best. Having these conversations in public is not a good idea. We should never be overly critical of a player in front of his peers. If it's going to be a difficult conversation, have it in the office. Also, find a time when you can block out your schedule, so that the conversation is not interrupted. Earmarking that time is a sign of respect to the other person.

  Our job requires that we give players immediate feedback on the field or court. The players expect it. Those coaching points need to be specific and delivered quickly. A wide-receiver coach who tells a player, "Don't drop the ball" is not helping him. In contrast, the coach who says, "Watch it into your hands before you begin to move upfield" is giving immediate, specific, and helpful feedback.

  Make your point and move on. We don't need a coaching clinic on the field. It is not an efficient use of time—we need the group to get reps, not come to a grinding halt, so that we can take a couple of minutes to explain something.

- *Plan.* Think beforehand about the message that you want to deliver, your choice of words, or even how you will react, if the other person gets upset. It's important to take the time to really consider what you are trying to accomplish and make sure that you are not "shooting from the hip."

  Having an outline before you start a meeting with a player or a member of the staff is a great way to keep yourself on point. It enables you to steer the conversation back to your feedback and/or your concerns, should it veer off course. We want to talk in specifics, not generalities. Having a plan for providing feedback allows us to do that.

- *Be timely—don't miss the teachable moment.* As coaches, we cannot miss the "teachable moment," because once we do, it is gone, and we can't get it back. If a mistake is made, and it is not addressed quickly, we are missing the opportunity to help the player get better. If you are recognizing a positive performance, you make a point by acknowledging it immediately and reinforcing why it was worth celebrating.

  Do not let things simmer. If something needs to be addressed, do it quickly. If a coach or player is upset, waiting to talk through the issue makes it difficult to continue moving forward in whatever we are doing. Bad news is not like wine; it does not get better with age!

- *Introduce the topic.* You should always be interested in being polite and professional, so normal greetings and check-ins at the beginning of the conversation are to be expected. After those, you ought to quickly introduce the topic, so that there is no ambiguity. It also allows the other person a moment to collect their thoughts. For example, "I appreciate you coming in to visit. I want to talk about yesterday's scrimmage. You had multiple mental errors and I am concerned about that. I want to figure out what's going on and how I can help you."
- *It's never personal.* When giving constructive criticism, it very important to remember that you are being critical of an action or a performance, not of a person. The coach must be able to separate the two and make sure that the other person never feels like they are being attacked as an individual.

  Today, with Generation Z, this factor is more important than ever. Being aware of the words we choose and how we place them in the coaching point is critical. There is a big difference between, "You are a soft player," and "That was a soft play." The best way to ensure that you never cross this line is to always frame the feedback in relationship to your standards. For example, "We pride ourselves on playing with physical toughness here, and that is not a physical play. That is not up to our standards."
- *Give it with care.* It's important to be sensitive to the other person and consider how your words are going to be received. A good bedside manner is a productive trait to have as a coach. Being honest does not mean being tactless.

  Too many coaches feel like because they are evaluating players and delivering feedback, they are allowed to do so in the way that makes them comfortable. As coaches and teachers, we must understand our audience. Each player's communication style is different, and we have to know how to talk to each person individually. A given style of sharing feedback might be effective for one player, and totally alienate another. We must know the difference.
- *Be specific.* If you want a performance or action to change, you should address it specifically. Speaking in generalities doesn't help anyone. It just creates confusion. Leaders must be crystal clear about what it is that they want corrected. "You are not playing well" is not a helpful statement for a player. "You are not playing well because you don't know your assignments and you are making too many mental mistakes. If you understood the offense better and knew who to block, I would feel more comfortable putting you on the field." That feedback is specific and makes it perfectly clear what the issue is and what needs to happen for it to be addressed.
- *Be balanced.* Whenever possible, you want to open these conversations with positive feedback. Acknowledge what the person does well and the ways they make a positive contribution to the team. If you start from a place of appreciation, the other person is more likely to accept the constructive criticism you are about to offer.

  With a player, I will always start with what they do well, before I begin discussing what they need to improve. Every single young person we work with does something well, and it is our job to recognize what that is and acknowledge it.

- *Speak for yourself.* You should never offer feedback that doesn't come directly from you or your observations. Referring to what anyone else might or might not think is simply hearsay, and it's reckless. It also shows a lack of courage. You should be willing to put your name, and your name alone, next to the feedback you are giving. Saying things like, "The whole staff thinks that you don't care about football" is bad form.
- *Include feelings.* You should express how you are feeling about the performance and/or the meeting but should allow the other person the same opportunity, as well. It provides an opportunity for you to show that they matter to you. As such, Gen Zers want to be a part of the discussion. For example, "I am disappointed about the choices that you are making off the field. It makes me feel like you are not invested in this team. Now that I have had the chance to discuss this with you, how are you feeling about it?"

  You can gain a lot of information from the player by allowing them to react to what has been talked about. Sometimes, you learn that they fully understand the point that was being made. Other times, you discover that you may not have done a good enough job, and they don't get from where you are coming.
- *Make feedback actionable.* This point is very important. You are of very little service, if all you do is point out where a person has fallen short. You must make sure that you are also laying out a plan of action in order for them to improve. This plan must include things that can be done immediately, as well as things that can be worked on over time.

  Telling a linebacker that he "has to do a better job of defeating blocks" is specific feedback, but it does not provide ways to fix the problem. "In the short-term, you need to use your hands more actively to get people off you. In the long-term, you need to get stronger in the weight room so that you can play with more power." Those statements are actionable. You are telling the player what he can do to help solve the problem.
- *Reframe.* At the end of the conversation, it always important to repeat and summarize what has been said. In some cases, it is a good idea to ask the other person to repeat back what they took from the conversation, so that you can understand if your message hit home. For example, in a one-on-one meeting with a player, finishing the conversation with a question like, "Tell me what we discussed here today" is a valuable tool.
- *Say thank you.* Any time that we share feedback with another person, we want the conversation to be professional. You should extend the other person every possible courtesy. Hearing constructive criticism is not easy and taking the time to simply say "thank you" acknowledges that and is sign of respect.

  No matter how difficult the conversation, when it is over, I will tell the player "Thank you for coming in to see me—I appreciate your time." I want to shake their hand, as well. I might be annoyed with them, or they might be angry with me, but I am going to make sure that they are treated with respect.

❑ S.B.I. Feedback Tool

The S.B.I. Feedback Tool stands for *situation/behavior/impact* and was developed by The Center for Creative Leadership. It serves as a roadmap for giving constructive criticism effectively. Its structure allows the listener to immediately understand the "what" and "why" of your comments. Also, by discussing the impact of their behavior, we give the listener the opportunity to think about and reflect on their action and how it affected other people. The following details how the S.B.I. Feedback tool would be applied:

- Situation:
  - ✓ Define the where and the when for your listener. It references a specific time and place and allows for some context.
  - ✓ Remind the listener what the expectation, standard, or goal was at the time.
  - ✓ For example, *"Last night, in the third quarter of the game, the punt-return unit was on the field, and our goal was to give the ball back to the offense."*
- Behavior:
  - ✓ Identify the action you observed that you want corrected.
  - ✓ Be specific.
  - ✓ Do not make subjective judgments.
  - ✓ For example, *"Instead of executing your block on the wing, you tried to rush and block the punt. As a result, you roughed the punter, we were called for a penalty, and the other team got the ball back."*
- Impact:
  - ✓ What impact did the observed behavior have?
  - ✓ How did the behavior affect you and others?
  - ✓ For example, *"I have concerns about putting you back out on the field, because I am not sure that you will play with the correct situational awareness."*
- Examples of S.B.I. feedback:
  - ✓ *"Elijah—you looked me in the eye on Friday in my office and told me that the paper was completed. Since then, the academic support staff has informed me that it is not finished. You have lied to me and now I have concerns about my ability to trust you."*
  - ✓ *"John—in Wednesday's meeting, we showed a clip and I told you that you could not hop around blocks on kick-off coverage. In yesterday's game, you did not take on the block and you jumped around it again. I have concerns about leaving you on this unit because I am not sure you will play physically enough."*

Feedback is such an instrumental part of effective communication and leadership, and it serves as a key ingredient in the development of relationships. Like many other parts of our lives, giving feedback is something that you can learn and improve upon with repetition. If you are going to be effective and impactful leader to Generation Z, the art of giving feedback needs to be valued, invested in, and practiced.

CHAPTER 10

Generation Z and Adversity

How often have you heard a grandparent utter the phrase, "They have no idea how easy they have it?"

It's not difficult to get someone from a previous generation to go on and on about how young people today don't face the same challenges they did. It is predictable and sometimes, almost comical. I can recall my father-in-law talking about having to work in his dad's gas station over the summer in order to earn money for school. My mother would remind us that a house in the suburbs was much better than an apartment in the city. Even older siblings want to make sure that their younger brothers and sisters understand it was harder for them. Remember the old line, "I had to walk to school, uphill, both ways?" It's memorable for a reason, because so many children heard it growing up. The message is made clear. Young people are told they have it much easier, and they're not as tough as those who preceded them. It's been that way for years.

It is too simplistic for older generations to look at those following them and declare it was easier, because they did not have the same hardships. It's not a gigantic leap to say that an 18-year-old who came of age in the 1960s faced different obstacles than someone the same age who is growing up in the world today. The environments that those two 18-year-olds experienced are so vastly different that it becomes impossible to offer a fair comparison. What makes life difficult in one era may not be applicable in another.

Growing up during the Vietnam War and being subject to the draft is an incredibly difficult thing to deal with, but so is growing up in the age of a global pandemic. Some facets of life are more difficult, and some are easier. More and more young people today are becoming "boomerang kids," they are moving home with their parents as they try to figure out what's next. Just because that is very different from previous generations, doesn't make it wrong. Every generation excels in some areas and falls short in others; however, they are all unique in their own ways.

The issue for Generation Z is that they have perception problem. Parents, employers, teachers, and coaches will gladly offer anecdotes about how kids today are not as gritty as they once were, that they are not able to handle even the smallest of difficulties. In our online world, rants about "snowflakes" and participation trophies can be found with the click of a button. Parenting styles used to raise this generation are studied and analyzed in academic settings, and often criticized.

Employers complain about young workers who do not want to pay their dues. Coaches in my own profession long for a time when two practices in a single day were acceptable and wish they had never heard the term "acclimatization period." We are all led to believe that young people today are socially incapable, emotionally fragile, and non-committed. Media, entertainment, politics, the Internet—they all portray and amplify a picture of Generation Z as being "soft" and not up to facing the obstacles that life is most certainly going to present. In short, the commonly accepted view is that they lack resilience, and therefore cannot deal with adversity.

Developing resilience is a critical step in a young person's transition into adulthood. To characterize an entire generation of not having enough of it is depressing and borders on scary. To imagine the future of our world in the hands of a group of people who are not capable of handling adversity is cause for some concern, to say the least. However, like most things in life, I believe that the truth lies somewhere in the middle. I believe that there are reasons people believe Generation Z cannot handle adversity, some of their own doing and some not. I believe that Generation Z has lived through some seminal moments in history that have helped/forced them to develop more resilience. And I believe there is more that we can do to help them to continue to learn how to cope with and persevere through difficult times.

❑ Why Can't Gen Z Handle Adversity?

Most experts agree the way Generation Z was raised has contributed to the fact they have difficulty dealing with adversity. As mentioned earlier, Millennials had "helicopter" parents who hovered over their every move and were there to quickly pick them up when they fell. Generation Z is being raised by "snowplow" parents. These parents do not stay close by to pick their child up after failure. Instead, they remove every obstacle in the child's way, so failure isn't even an option. As a result, these youngsters never really understand what adversity is until later in life. A "snowplow" parent yells at the Little League coach, blames the teacher for what they consider poor grades, bribes college admissions officers (e.g., the Varsity Blues scandal), and believes that it is the manager's fault that their child is unhappy at work. The differences between these two styles of parenting are dramatic.

Young people today are also the first generation of kids who were brought inside, put on screens, and monitored. When I was a growing up, there was no such thing as a "playdate." Not only were we not monitored, but we were also kicked out of our homes, when the weather was nice! It was not uncommon to hear a mom in the neighborhood say, "It's gorgeous outside. Go play and don't come back until dinner time." That is almost unheard of now.

Generation Z lost the independence to go out and learn for themselves. They missed out on the adventures with friends, the fear of getting lost in the woods, the pain of a badly scraped knee, and the lessons in winning and losing that comes with "pick-up" sports. They lost opportunities to handle difficulty and deal with disappointment.

The best teacher is experiencem and Gen Zers missed some of thatm because of how overly protective their parents were.

Dr. Jonathan Haidt, a social psychologist and professor at NYU's Stern School of Business, articulated his concern succinctly, when he said, "the country is facing rising rates of anxiety, depression, and fragility among today's teens and college students, many of whom have been surrounded by protective adults their entire lives. What will happen when they enter the 'real world,' where the protections will be far fewer and the demand far greater?"

Additionally, the educational atmosphere that Generation Z has matriculated through is far different and has had a negative effect on them. Again, they have come of age in a time when information has never been easier to find. They are born in a digital-era and have access to a vast array of knowledge that would have been considered impossible only 30 years ago. That has been to their advantage. However, changes to education, parents that have become too involved and too demanding, and a sense of academic entitlement have created several challenges for Gen Zers as well.

Schools and teachers are being judged by test scores, which has altered the way that they approach students. Parents have made themselves too involved, often demanding better grades for their children and blaming the schools for shortcom ngs. High school students are allowed re-takes and feel they are "owed" grades. Too many of them view "B" and "C" level work as failing. Standardized test scores and college admissions are highly competitive and have become big business. None of these things are helping to prepare Generation Z for the next step. Faculty in colleges across the country are reporting increasing numbers of students who not only respond poorly to criticism, but also feel entitled to multiple opportunities on exams and assignments. Things that were once considered simply challenging in the classroom have now become insurmountable obstacles.

The Internet and social media are partly to blame for the notion that Generation Z cannot handle adversity. That blame is based both in fact and in fiction. What young people see online effects how they feel about the world around them, their peers, and themselves. Studies have shown that heavy use of social media, particularly among girls, has some relationship to anxiety and depression. They are seeing other people's lives through a rose-colored lens and trying to live up to a standard that is based in a false reality.

In addition, a lot of what they see, listen to, and interact with is dark. Information and images from across the world expose kids to horror and tragedy in a way they have never been before. In our world today, terrorists post videos on YouTube of beheadings. All of that can be difficult to process for a young person and become too heavy a burden to bear. There is a lot of negativity out there that can beat a person down and cause them to lose hope.

On the other hand, social media has created a false narrative around Generation Z. Young people today are far more likely to express themselves honestly and openly on social media. It is not uncommon to see a Gen Zer post on Instagram, Snapchat, or

Twitter and allow themselves to be totally truthful and vulnerable. They will speak freely about how they are feeling, whether those feelings be positive or negative. A "crying selfie" is not unusual at all. Older generations tend to roll their eyes at that honesty and view it as a sign of weakness. I think that is fiction. Just because a young person will share, out loud for all to see, that they are facing some sort of adversity does not mean they aren't willing or equipped to take it on.

That leads us to mental health. We referenced earlier, there is a mental health crisis among young people in America today. The number of men and women in Generation Z who report struggling with mental health issues is staggering. Depression, anxiety, self-harm, and suicide are all on the rise within this group. The journal JAMA Pediatrics reported that one in seven children and young adults today struggle with a mental health condition. When we look back at the world that Gen Zers are growing up in, it is easy to understand why they are anxious—there has been plenty to be anxious about. Given these challenges, should we be surprised that it has been difficult for them to develop and display resilience?

With that said, Generation Z has helped remove some of the stigma attached to mental health issues. They are far more open to talking about it and more willing to seek help than any generation before. They are also far more proactive about mental health. They talk about self-care and ways to improve their mental and emotional well-being. Gen Z's willingness to acknowledge the importance of mental health and seek help are signs of maturity and development and will help them better deal with adversity later in life.

Social media has created a false narrative around Generation Z.

❑ Generation Z Is Generation "Resilient"

Each generation has lived through some sort of pivotal moment in history, admittedly some more important than others. The Greatest Generation came of age during the Depression and were the primary participants in World War II. History has shown they helped shape our country for decades to come. There are mountains of information about how those events affected the men and women who experienced those incredible challenges. Economic instability, job loss, the threat of war—those things, along with many others, forced young people in that era to face harsh realities and develop resiliency. I cannot think of much greater adversity than trying to survive the depression and then being drafted into the military.

Baby Boomers dealt with the Vietnam War and dramatic social change across the country. Generation X grew up amid the Cold War and an energy crisis. Millennials faced a world that changed significantly right in front of them due to unbelievable advances in technology and they lived through the Attacks of September 11th. Each generation of people saw their environment change dramatically and they were forced to adjust and overcome. I believe the same factor holds true for Generation Z—they have experienced changes and challenges in their time that have shaped who they are and helped them develop a toughness that so many think they lack.

According to The Center for Generational Kinetics, a generational research company and their 2020 survey *The State of Gen Z*, we don't have to look very far to find the most significant hurdle faced by Gen Zers. "Based on our research at CGK, we believe the COVID 19 pandemic is the most formative generation-defining moment that has shaped Gen Z at this critical time in their transition into adulthood. As a result, they are reporting much higher rates of anxiety, stress, decreased work hours, unemployment, and the need for financial help."

For Generation Z, the pandemic disrupted nearly every part of their lives. Those on the younger end of the spectrum lost the ability to go to school in person. Many of them struggled with the transition to online education and/or schools were poorly equipped to handle distance learning. Social development was slowed, as daily interpersonal interactions were made impossible because of isolation and social distancing. Young children dealt with the loss of loved ones and tried to understand why saying goodbye was not an option.

For the Gen Zers in the middle, some of the most important times of their lives in high school were adversely affected. Over half of those polled in the *State of Gen Z* said they had an overall negative experience with online learning, and 61 percent said they much rather have in-person classes. They went without athletics, musicals and plays, proms, and even graduations. Standardized tests were cancelled, and the college application process became more confusing. College itself became more complicated. Young people and their families were forced to weigh the cost of college versus what had become an online model at a lot of institutions across the country. Many of them were forced to move back home despite plans of being away at school.

For the oldest members of Gen Z, they could not have tried to enter the workforce at a more difficult time. Jobs were evaporating across the country, wages were being reduced, job descriptions were changing, and lay-offs often involved those newest to the company ("last in, first out"). At a point in their lives when Gen Zers were supposed to be forming their professional identities, they were thrust into a world that was being thrown completely up-side down.

Like those who came before them, Generation Z has faced down their seminal moment and grown as a result. Greg Lukianoff, co-author of *"The Coddling of the American Mind"* and president of the Foundation for Individual Rights in Education, says, "There is a real possibility for a generation that has been told that they are more fragile than they actually are, and they are less resilient than they actually are, that facing genuine scary adversity and getting through it will actually be quite empowering."

Most young people today feel that they have been changed by the pandemic, and the majority believe they will be better off for it. They are using the experience as an opportunity to plan, engage, and work for a better future. According to Michelle Parmelee, Deloitte Global Chief People and Purpose Officer and their *2020 Deloitte Global Millennial Survey,* "Despite uncertain and discouraging conditions, Millennials and Gen Zs express impressive resiliency and resolve to improve the world. As we rebuild our economies and society, young people will be critical in shaping the world that emerges."

The signs of Gen Z's resiliency in the face of adversity and the resulting growth are all around us. They have changed and evolved in many different parts of their lives. First and foremost, they care more about other people. As a high number of young people were forced to move back home, they grew closer and more concerned about the parents and grandparents. They also started to care more about their communities. Over 85 percent of college students said that they have a better appreciation for the difficulties of others because of the pandemic. Having to witness the suffering of loved ones, neighbors, and society, in general, affected Generation Z.

As a result, Gen Zers have become a very empathetic generation. They recognize the importance of people coming together to help and support one another. They also understand that despite all the wealth in our country and advances in technology, that there are millions of people who are still struggling in meaningful ways, and they feel that deeply.

Generation Z used the pandemic as a time of self-discovery. Faced with all this new-found free time, young people had to choose between indulging in nonsense and wasting it or putting it to good use. Most took advantage of the time and used it as an opportunity to discover and then more clearly define themselves as people. Nearly 90 percent reported using the time to express themselves creatively. Another 60 percent used the time to pick up a new hobby with fitness, cooking, writing, and playing a musical instrument being the most popular. For a generation that has a reputation for being glued to their devices, Gen Zers got outside and enjoyed nature. In general, they slowed down a bit and took a breath. The beauty in all of this is that the self-reflection, the new hobbies, the creativity, the getting out of the house—none if it was done on a deadline, for a grade, or for a resume. It was organic, and it was about personal growth.

The pandemic altered the way Generation Z looks at money and employment, as well. According the CGK survey, 59 percent say they will be more intentional about saving money because of COVID 19. They experienced, firsthand, the financial strain that it placed on themselves and their families. As a result, they are financially responsible in the way that they budget and save. They are going to be more prepared, if a crisis like this should ever happen again.

Many young people began to reexamine their career paths. With at least 30 percent of jobs eliminated during the pandemic not expected to return, their future lies in an unrecognizable and unpredictable economy. The traditional path to employment and what has defined success have given way to more uncommon view of careers. For example, trades that were once seen as a step below a college education are now viewed as increasingly valuable because of demand and pay scale.

A friend in the construction industry shared with me that skilled labor is incredibly difficult to find, and they are earning top dollar. Twenty-five years ago, being an electrician may have been looked down upon by some people, but that isn't the case for young people today. In addition to embracing things like skilled labor, Gen Zers are also more likely to create their own paths in terms of their careers. They are willing to go against convention and carve out their own niche. They are interested in working from home and at different times of the day. This creativity and willingness to think outside of the box is going to yield new ideas, new processes, and new technology that will change the world.

While the pandemic is the defining moment for Generation Z, it is clearly not the only impactful one. Living through COVID 19 has made Gen Z more empathetic and that empathy has drawn them closer to the social justice and environmental movements. They feel their involvement in these causes is a personal calling—they are taking their trauma and changing it into purpose. Because they are more in tune with the needs and struggles of others, they will not stand idle in the face of racism, political corruption, gun violence, the treatment of women, or the degradation of the environment. Generation Z is pushing for change. Across the world we see young people leading protests, igniting debate, effecting policy, and fostering diversity.

They are also utilizing social media as an outlet to amplify their voices, gather groups together, and to keep people informed in real time. Growing up in the digital era has provided them with a platform to which no previous generation had access. Their message can reach millions in a matter of hours. There is power in numbers, and Gen Zers understand that.

❑ Guiding Gen Z Through Adversity

When you move to a new part of the country, there are always people willing to help educate you about what makes that particular place unique. My family's move to Louisiana was no different. When we arrived in Baton Rouge, everyone we spoke with talked about preparing for hurricane season.

Now, we are not rookies. We have experienced weather events before. We've lived in Buffalo, NY, for heaven's sake—we have seen lake effect snow pile up and blow around to the point where it cripples an entire city for a week. We have hidden from the heat of Texas, felt the bone-chilling polar vortex of northern Indiana, ducked the tropical storms of Florida, and much more. However, what we have learned is while our experience might give us some sense of what might come, we will never truly be prepared, unless we heed the advice of those around us. We must listen to the people who know. You want to have a generator, food and water on hand, the ability to board up the windows, and a place to go in case of evacuation. In southern Louisiana, hurricanes are serious business, and the locals who have been through them can you help put together a plan.

Sergey Tinyakov/Shutterstock.com

We all face challenges in life; how we react to them is our individual choice.

When it comes to dealing with adversity, we (parents, managers, teachers, and coaches) are the locals who possess the insight, and Generation Z is new in town. They have developed some knowledge through experience, but they need help as well. We can guide them and help them develop a better plan for dealing with difficult times and growing tougher in the process. The following are some of the ways we can do that:

- *Relationships first.* It should be no surprise that I believe our interactions with Generation Z should start from a place of building a meaningful relationship. When young people are loved, they are more likely to develop resilience. Our best chance to connect and positively influence them is if we start by showing an honest interest in their lives. We cannot be of any service to them if they don't trust us, and they won't trust us, unless we know who they are and where they come from.
- *Perfection is not the goal.* Anthony Rostain, co-director of the Adult ADHD Treatment and Research Program and co-author of *The Stressed Years of Their Lives: Helping Your Kid Survive and Thrive During Their College Years*, feels the pursuit of perfection creates an all-or-nothing line of thinking and makes it difficult to face challenges and accept disappointment. He says, "Today's world may be a more competitive and less forgiving place, but when that assessment yields a constructed definition of personal success, it fans the flames of destructive perfectionism. It is vital to remember how varied the paths are to a happy and successful life." There is a perception for young people that they need to be perfect, and when they fall short, it can lead them to feel incompetent. "Perfect" is impossible to attain, and we need to remind Gen Zers of that.
- *It's necessary to fail.* If perfection is impossible, then we must help young people understand that failure is not only inevitable, but also necessary to learn how to handle adversity. Like the immune system needs to be exposed to bacteria and viruses to develop a defense against them, the human spirit needs to understand what it is to fail in the face of difficulty. Failure is scary, but the experience will help develop the resilience needed to overcome in the future.
- *Self-regulation.* We all face challenges in life; how we react to them is our individual choice. When things get difficult, people will cope differently. Drugs and alcohol, food, video games, social media—there are any number of negative ways that can be used as an escape from a harsh reality. However, we can help young people learn and utilize skills to help them deal with adverse times. From basics like breathing skills, to venting frustration through exercise, to simply trying to always find the silver lining—we can show them how to keep themselves regulated during times of stress. A great first step is teaching them to "control the controllables." There is no sense dwelling on people or things that are out of our control.
- *Life is about nuance.* Our world has become increasingly polarized in recent years, and that has led to the idea that life is a battle between "us" and "them." Generation Z must learn that life is not black and white; in fact, life is mostly about shades of gray. We must help them understand that polarized thinking removes any room for nuance, and life is all about nuance. We need our young people to be critical thinkers and secure enough to know that someone can challenge their ideas, without attacking their identity as a person.

- *Develop confidence.* It's not a surprise to learn that some of the most successful people are often the most confident ones. People who consider themselves capable are more likely to persevere. Gen Zers need a confidence boost—they need to feel capable of handling adversity when they face it. I am not talking about inspiring talks; I am talking about preparation. We need to prepare young people for the adversity that they are going to face and help them to develop the specific tools to deal with it. In doing so, we give them the confidence to know they are ready when hard times come.

I find it a little disingenuous and frustrating when people characterize Generation Z as incapable of resilience. We know that the differences in the way they were raised, educated, and advances in technology they were exposed to made it easy to perceive them as entitled and weak. All that said, we cannot ignore all they have seen and been through. Gen Z has never known a world at peace. They have lived through a pandemic, economic upheaval, gun violence, social unrest, and a worsening climate crisis. In fact, they have endured more adversity than any generation has in over seven decades.

All of this pain and suffering could have crushed them. It could have sapped their energy and destroyed their resolve. Instead, they have grown and come out stronger. They have toughened, built-up calluses, and are developing a common-sense approach to life. Generation Z has proven to be more determined than ever to improve the world that they live in. They want to make society a better place.

Young people today are resilient. They have faced down incredible adversity and emerged bruised, but hopeful and ready to make a positive impact in the world. Instead of pointing out their differences and deficiencies, we need to gather around them, love them, and guide them along the way.

CHAPTER 11

Valued Perspectives

We can gain a great deal of wisdom from the perspectives and experiences of other people. This chapter features some thoughts on relationships from coaches across the country whom I have to come to know and admire. This group of incredible people is different in a number of ways. They come from all over the country. It includes men and women. They work at the high school level, in college, and in the professional ranks. And their expertise lies in football, basketball, softball, baseball, and lacrosse. What they have in common is a unique ability to build relationships with their athletes and guide them to success, on and off the field. I am extremely grateful for their generosity and blessed to call them friends.

❑ Chuck Kyle—Head Football Coach, St. Ignatius High School (OH)

Chuck Kyle has dedicated decades of his life, serving the young men of his alma mater, St. Ignatius High School in Cleveland, Ohio. Coach Kyle served as head football coach for 40 years. In that time, the Wildcats became a household name for fans of prep football. He led the program to the state playoffs 29 times, has won 11 state championships, and three national championships. Coach Kyle also served as the head coach for the track and field program for 46 seasons and led his teams to two state titles in that sport, as well. Widely considered one of the greatest coaches in Ohio history, Coach Kyle was recognized as the state coach of the year on four occasions and was inducted into the Greater Cleveland Sports Hall of Fame in 2010.

If human beings were animals, we would travel in herds. We humans innately realize that we cannot make it alone. Even Jesus Christ needed the 12 Apostles. We mostly live in towns and cities, places where we are close to others. Most of our enjoyable experiences occur while socializing with other people. I think that is why we find it sad, when we learn of an individual who eats or attends a movie alone.

History shows that human beings get so much more done while working together with others. There are many examples of individuals spending more time volunteering to help others than spending time on the job. Being involved and concerned with other people is therapeutic. Having a good relationship with someone is mentally and spiritually fulfilling. Having a good relationship with many people may be heaven.

American philosopher/poet Ralph Waldo Emerson wrote in depth about the central building block of human relationship; he called it "OVERSOUL"—"a unity within which every man's particular being is contoured and made one with all other: a common heart that is a vital force in the universe in which all souls participate and that therefore transcends individual consciousness." (I teach American literature, so I teach Emerson every year.) A newborn baby is very self-centered. As the child matures, he/she becomes more aware of other people. How important is it that the child starts to understand that some of the same feelings, desires, goals and values are shared by others? As that happens, Emerson is somewhere smiling—"Oversoul."

RELATIONSHIPS ARE THE GREATEST MOTIVATION

I will never disparage a person for setting individual goals; a human being needs to visualize becoming successful within his/her chosen endeavor and take pride in the effort used to gain that success. Pride in oneself is a virtue, as long as it is controlled by humility—Greek, Roman, and Shakespearean tragedy consistently presents the FATAL FLAW of hubris—selfish pride.

So, individual goals are good, but what is THE GREATEST MOTIVATION? Fame? Fortune? History shows those can be profitable, but rather empty. Look carefully at the lift of spirit created by RELATIONSHIPS.

History shows that human beings get so much more done while working together with others..

My father-in-law studied to become a lawyer at John Carroll University and was set to go to law school. On December 7, 1941, he had dinner over his girlfriend's house and volunteered to walk up to the corner store to buy a couple of after-dinner cigars. In his coat pocket was an engagement ring; his plan was to ask his girlfriend's father for permission to marry when he returned to the house and celebrate in a manly way with his soon to be father-in-law. As he entered the corner store, the radio was blaring memorable worldly news: the Japanese had bombed Pearl Harbor. My father-in-law volunteered a few days later. He married his girlfriend ten days before being shipped out. He entered the Army Air Corps training to become a navigator. He promised his new wife he would not try to be a hero—he would come back alive.

He trained to navigate a B-17 bomber. The crew he trained with came from various areas of the country and began their relationship with little connection other than the plane and the hope to survive.

That crew flew 28 bombing missions, witnessing most of the other crews going down in flames. With his crew by his side in that B-17, my father-in-law was the lead navigator on the first daytime bombing of Berlin: over one thousand planes would set their course, based on my father-in-law's calculations. That B-17 limped back across the English Channel several times, but miraculously, my father-in-law and the crew survived and came home alive.

Years later, I finally asked my father-in-law was he ever scared during those raids. I will never forget his answer; it had a profound effect on my life. He turned to me and said, "I was scared—frightened out of my mind. But, I would look to my left, and I would look to my right, and would see the other guys in the crew, and I knew I could not let them down." It was not patriotism or the national anthem that carried him in those extremely intense, close moments; it was the relationship my father-in-law had with guys he had known for only less than a year that gave him the courage and strength to rise above natural fear.

In the game of football, in the fourth quarter during a tight game, it is not the band playing the fight song or the crowd cheering wildly that motivates those eleven guys in the huddle. Each of them "looks to his left, and looks to his right and sees the other guys on the team, and decides not to let them down."

That is why football is such a great game of RELATIONSHIPS.

❑ Marv Levy—Former NFL, CFL, and College Head Coach

Marv Levy had a coaching career that spanned over five decades and saw him work with players at the high school, college, and professional levels. He is a 1943 graduate of South Shore High School in Chicago, and following school, he enlisted in the Army and served in WWII. Upon returning home, Coach Levy enrolled at Coe College in Iowa, where he lettered in football, basketball, and track. He then went on to earn a graduate degree from Harvard. His coaching career began at St. Louis Country Day and then took him back to Coe, on to New Mexico, Cal, and William and Mary. Marv then entered the NFL as one of the first special teams coaches in the league. Stops with the Eagles, Rams, and Redskins led to the opportunity to become the head coach of the Montreal Alouettes of the CFL. There, he won two Grey Cups. He later became the head coach of the Kansas City Chiefs and the Buffalo Bills, whom he led to a record four straight Super Bowls. Coach Levy was enshrined in the Pro Football Hall of Fame in 2001 and has authored five books since his retirement.

One of the greatest satisfactions I had during my 47-year-long coaching career was getting to know so many people, whose values, whose knowledge, whose abilities, whose personalities, whose opinions, whose work ethics and so much more have had such an uplifting impact on my life. I will always treasure those opportunities!

Like them, I loved the game. I also loved the high values that I feel could be derived from my association with those of them who exhibited admirable qualities and who exhibited how much they cared for their cohorts, their game-day opponents, the fans who brought such enthusiasm to the game, and the media who conveyed so much of it to those fans, and yes, often times (but not always) back to us coaches.

There are so many lifetime friends, whether they be players, coaching partners, coaching rivals, team owners, front-office personnel, fans, members of the media, and many more whom I feel so fortunate to have come to know and respect during my coaching career. I loved the game, and so did they.

❑ Brick Haley—Defensive Line—Purdue University Football

Brick Haley is a 33-year veteran of coaching and has worked at the high school, college, and NFL levels. He is recognized as one of the top defensive line coaches in football and has guided national statistic leaders and all-conference players throughout his career. He has been a key component on staffs at Enterprise HS (AL), Austin Peay, Troy, Houston, Clemson, Baylor, Georgia Tech, Mississippi State, the Chicago Bears, LSU, Texas, Missouri, and Purdue. He has been a member of teams that have won three conference championships, including the 2011 SEC championship with LSU. He has also coached in nine bowl games, including the 2012 BCS National Championship Game. A graduate of and star player at Alabama A&M, Brick was inducted into his alma mater's Hall of Fame in 2005. He and his wife, Tina, started the Brick Road to Success foundation to raise awareness of autism.

Growing up in Gadsden, Alabama, I knew that education and football would be my way of supporting my family. I received a scholarship at Alabama A&M to play football. I had a tremendous amount of success on the football field as a player, and I'm humbled to be an inductee into their Hall of Fame. However, it was the education I received and the relationships I formed that changed my life forever. That's exactly what has allowed me to coach this game for over 30 years, the relationships with my players.

I'm a firm believer in, "they don't care how much you know, till' they know how much you care." I love every single young man who has ever played for me, and they are members of my family. Just like with any family, you have tough moments. That's when our young men need us most. When life presents them with adversity, it's my hope that they are prepared to tackle those problems with solutions, just like we do on the football field. That is my purpose, above all, to prepare these young men for life after football. I believe in always being honest and truthful with all my players. And sometimes, that includes uncomfortable conversations, for them to hear things they don't want to hear, but need to hear. I believe I owe every young man the truth. The relationships are truly the reward. The building blocks of the relationships are trust and respect. The relationships are my "why" for coaching this great game of football.

❑ Deanna Gumpf—Head Softball Coach, University of Notre Dame

Deanna Gumpf has guided for the softball program at Notre Dame for 21 seasons and has over 700 victories on her resume, making her one of the elite head coaches in the country. Under her guidance, the Fighting Irish have appeared in 17 NCAA Regionals and won 11 conference regular season or tournament championships. Deanna and her coaches are highly regarded by their peers, having been named National Fastpitch Coaches Association Regional Coaching Staff of the Year five times. She has also excelled in player development, having 17 players recognized as NFCA All-Americans, six conference players of the year, four conference pitchers of the years, and two conference freshman of the year. Her Notre Dame teams have excelled in regards to community service, as well. In 2011, they started Strike Out Cancer and have raised over $250,000 for South Bend Memorial Children's Hospital. A graduate of Nebraska, Deanna was a 2x-All Big Eight player. She went on to receive a master's degree from Azusa Pacific and served as assistant at Long Beach St.

If you asked me 24 years ago why I got into coaching, I would have told you that I love the game, love to compete, and love to win. What I've learned over the past 24 years is yes, I love the game and competing, but that is not the reason that I have stayed in coaching, and those are not the things that drive me every day. In the beginning, all that seemed to matter was the external scoreboard and measuring myself against wins and losses. However, I've realized that my internal scoreboard is really everything that truly matters to me and is what drives me every single day. It consists of all the stuff that matters long after the games are over. This includes my relationships with my players, our team culture, my behaviors on and off the field, and doing the right thing. It also consists of my coaching staff and the dynamic we share. A huge part of my internal scoreboard is also my relationships with my alumni. Nothing brings me more satisfaction than watching them succeed and building lifelong connections with them. The ultimate win is when alumni come back to visit Notre Dame to watch the team play, and they hang around the stadium or join my family and me in my backyard for dinner.

The realization of my internal scoreboard has resulted in my staff changing the way we coach our players. I have realized that we have to work just as hard off the field, managing relationships, as we do on the field with hitting, pitching, and fielding balls. Communication and team culture have become the top priority. Managing relationships and building trust have become a part of our practices. I truly believe that coaching has become more enjoyable to me, since our staff has shifted our priorities. I truly get to know and understand our players. I believe I am at Notre Dame today because of this shift in our priorities. I have committed to taking the time outside of practice to spend time with players through one-on-one meetings. Our goal is to spend time together to get to know their dreams, and work to try to help each player fulfill them.

Once I realized what drove me in the game, I became a better coach. Of course, I get tears in my eyes when a player hits her first homerun or a pitcher hurls a great game, but I am more proud of them graduating from this special university or when they share with me something amazing happening in their lives. The bonds I get to build every year have shaped who I am and drive me to be the best person I can possibly be for all those who come in contact with my program. Throughout all my years of coaching, the wins on the field simply do not compare to the value of the relationships.

❑ Scott Fitch—Head Basketball Coach, Fairport HS (NY)

Scott Fitch has been the head coach at Fairport High School, outside of Rochester, NY, since 2001, and has won over 300 games in his 20 years with the program. Five times, he was honored as the Monroe County Coach of the Year, twice the Section V Coach of the Year, and once (2007) Greater Rochester Coach of the Year. He led the Red Raiders to back-to-back Section V championships in 2006 and 2007, and to the state final-four in 2007. He has also been a coach for the USA Basketball program since 2017. Coach Fitch served as head coach for the 2019 USA Nike Hoop Summit and served as an assistant for the 2018 USA Men's U17 World Cup team and the 2017 USA Men's U16 National Team.

After college, I was playing pro basketball and trying to figure out my direction—I was living with the uncertainty of not knowing what league or country I would be in next. It was an exciting time in my life, but also one filled with many questions. My Dad, Jeff Fitch, is a legendary coach at Fairport High School, winning over 450 games in his career. One evening, I joined him and a number of his former players for dinner and couple of drinks. I listened to story after story about things that happened during their careers and life lessons they learned from my Dad. I saw the impact my Dad had on them. Not only on the court, but more importantly, off it. I then started to think about how many lives he had impacted this way. I wanted to do that. I decided that night I wanted to be a coach.

Relationships are why I got into coaching, but they are also why kids play hard and compete. They are why players commit so much time, effort, and energy. I think relationships are essential for team chemistry. For a player to fully engage in a "team-first mentality," he must have relationships with coaches and teammates he cares about. If he does not have those meaningful relationships, he will not feel the need to put the team first.

There is a huge need for the kids whom we work with to have real relationships. Most of their relationships are weak and technology-driven. That is why you see the suicide rate so high. I feel they are yearning for real relationships, even if they do not know it. I enjoy listening to them. Letting them share their thoughts and have a voice. I like letting them be a part of the process (e.g.,when we are setting up our off-season plan to get better or style of play we will use to maximize our personnel, etc.). It gives them ownership. When they have ownership, they invest.

When we talk about building relationships, we focus on trust, truth, and care. I think these three ingredients are essential. You have to earn the trust of your players and coaches. You do that by being honest and consistent. I think they need to know you care about them (coaches and players). They need to know you care about your vision and goals. The passion I have for our players and what we stand for is contagious.

Building relationships with our players demands one thing—effort. Relationships don't just happen. A number of years ago, I was talking to a wrestling coach at Spencerport HS—they had a storied wrestling program in New York State. He said he took the time to call a couple kids every night to connect with them and just check in. They had about 50 kids on the team! I could not believe it. As a result, I started calling kids throughout the week or having a couple kids stay after practice every day. I look forward to these one-on-one interactions. We talk about some basketball, but usually we try to talk about other things as well, about life in general. It is incredible what has come up in these conversations—mental issues, family members passing away, etc. It is amazing to me that if I did not have those conversations, I would have never known some of these things were going on. How can we ask a kid to perform at a high level and be present for our practice or game, when they may be dealing with a personal issue that is dominating their thoughts?

High-level communication is a key. That means being able to communicate in a heated moment—knowing the same language, able to be honest and to the point. To have this, you need to create an environment in which everyone feels safe to share their thoughts. They have to know they will be respected. Everyone is expected to be engaged and committed to interacting. At USA Basketball, we talk about having an ecosystem that fosters this. I believe in debriefing often. I love the way the Navy Seals debrief with honesty, fostering the ability to improve in their next operation. Rod Olson uses the "3-2-1" method—three things we did really well, two things we can improve on, and one thing we can learn. I use this method in many ways—after a drill, film session, game, etc. This also allows you to get use to constructive criticism, something that I have learned to yearn for and welcome. We maintain a positive feel, because we are starting with three things we did well, and we outnumber the positive with negative. Lastly, we are always looking to learn and grow—individually and as a unit.

Working with USA Basketball, one thing I have learned about the elite players in the country is how they love to be pushed. I really enjoy their competitiveness. Maybe more importantly, I have learned how they need to be told the truth. Most of these players are surrounded by "yes" people. Their entourage is often looking to get something from that elite athlete. These young men are rarely told the truth. They need to hear it though, in order to improve as basketball players and grow as people.

I did not get into coaching to win games or championships; I got into coaching to build relationships and impact lives. The player/coach relationship is more important now more than ever, and I am working every day to stay connected and positively impact my players.

❑ Cheston Blackshear—Tight Ends/Tackles Coach—Dartmouth College Football

Cheston Blackshear has taken his experiences as a player at the highest levels of college football and transferred them into a successful career coaching. A high-school All-American at Ed White HS (FL), he was the first offensive lineman ever named Florida Times-Union Player of the Year. Cheston went on to the University of Florida, where he was an All-SEC player and a member of the Gator's 1997 National Championship team. He graduated in 2000 and was awarded the Fergie Ferguson Award, honoring a senior player who displayed the most character, courage, and leadership. After two years in pro football, Cheston entered the coaching ranks and spent time at Florida, Illinois, Columbia, New Mexico, Georgetown, Nevada, and Dartmouth. He's been instrumental in the development of a number of all-conference players and has built a reputation as a coach who can help a player get every ounce out of his ability.

The player/coach relationship is more important now more than ever.

As coaches, we all know building and maintaining relationships with our student-athletes is vital. It's essentially our lifeline during the recruiting process and continues to grow during their time at our school. When you ask someone what the essential elements to building a good relationship is they will likely rattle off buzz words like honesty, respect, and open communication. This is true. We do need those pieces, but as I sit here thinking about what makes a relationship truly matter, make it impactful and meaningful, we have to go beyond buzz words and dig deeper. We have to go farther and be willing to do the work.

The recent pandemic and social injustice events have positioned us to do this work. We are having real and open conversations about student-athletes' experiences and how they are feeling. At times, it can be uncomfortable, but it is bringing us closer and creating a safe space to talk. In the past, I've had some of my Black players tell me the advice they were told in order to "fit in," and it's disturbing but considered to be the norm in some communities. "Don't wear du rags or braids and take out your earrings." "Always smile when you pass a white person, no matter how bad your day is."

What I found is that at no point, was anyone asking them how they feel. How are they doing adjusting to the team or campus? Essentially, they had to adjust to the white majority, and their voice didn't matter. Who they are as a young Black man was becoming lost.

As a Black male, I understand their feelings. I was given similar advice growing up from my mom and dad, before I left for college. Even today, in my professional world, I have to play the game to fit in. But, maybe it's time for a new game. I have the responsibility to all of my student-athletes to help them be heard. Their voices are important to me, and I will use my platform as a coach to help develop them beyond the field. I know not every relationship will be the same, because every young man's needs are different, but I am committed to building quality relationships that will make us better on and off the field.

In the past, I've made the mistake of not cultivating relationships with my student athletes beyond recruiting, so I know I need to really listen and invest in the student-athletes in front of me. I'll also learn where my student-athletes come from and what they hope to achieve. We will build confidence in one another by being open and honest about our experiences and talk about how I can help him grow. My goal is to make sure my guys know they can come to me for anything, and I will provide guidance that has their best interest in mind. In essence, building relationships with my players is a privilege and something I'm grateful for with each new class of young men.

❑ Paul Mainieri—Former Head Baseball Coach, Louisiana State University

Paul Mainieri is the proto-typical coach's kid, having grown up on the baseball diamonds of south-Florida with his father, legendary junior college coach, Demie Mainieri. He started his head-coaching career at St. Thomas University in Florida where he coached for six seasons. He then took over at Air Force, where he also remained for six seasons and left as the second winningest coach in program history. In 1995, Paul took over the Notre Dame baseball program, and it became a model of consistency. Under his watch, the Irish appeared in nine NCAA tournaments and qualified for the College World Series in 2002. In 2007, he took over SEC power LSU and has appeared in four College World Series, winning the national title in 2009. Coach Mainieri has been named a conference coach of the year three times, national coach of the year twice, and has been inducted into the American Baseball Coaches Association Hall of Fame.

Growing up the son of a legendary junior college baseball coach, I had the fortunate opportunity to get a solid grasp on why to enter the coaching profession. My father, at his retirement, after 30 years at Miami-Dade Community College, was generally regarded as the greatest junior college baseball coach in history. He was the first JUCO coach to win over 1000 games in his career, won a national championship (with five other near misses at the JUCO World Series), and prepared 30 players to eventually play in the major leagues. In other words, he experienced unprecedented success as a coach.

However, when I, as a 14-year-old, informed my father that I knew I wanted to enter the coaching profession, when my playing career was over, he gave me just one bit of advice. He sternly told me that if I were to go into the profession, I should do it for the right reasons. The incorrect reasons, as he stated to me, would be to go into it for the money, for the prestige, for the love of sports, or the desire to win. Rather, go into the profession if you want to impact young people's lives in a positive way. He went on to say that coaches are first and foremost teachers and that the lessons you teach your athletes to be successful on the fields of play will be the same qualities they will need to be successful later on in life in whatever endeavor they so choose.

Going into coaching armed with my father's advice, I realized that the only way your athletes would accept your lessons is if they firmly believed in what you were saying to them. They needed to trust you as a person, before they could trust you as a coach. Once the relationship you developed with your athletes was based on the truth at all times, whether the truth was good news or bad for a specific athlete, they respected and believed what you told them. I have a little saying I tell my players, "You cannot like the decision…and still respect the decision-maker." In order for an athlete to respect a coach, they have to believe that the coach wants to see them succeed and will do whatever he can to help them to success. That he believes in them and his expectations for them are simply for them to become the best player they are capable of being. And that the coach will always be honest with them.

I am proud that after 38 years of coaching, I still maintain relationships with so many former players. My day is not complete, until I've heard from at least one of those guys. When a former player expresses how my coaching helped mold them into the man he has become, it is incredible. When one of them tells me how much I have done for him and thanks me for the time I dedicated to his development as a person, I realize that my father was right all those years ago. When I hear those words from a former player, that is my greatest reward. That is more important to me than anything.

❑ Jill Phillips—Former Head Women's Basketball Coach, Princeton High School (OH)

Jill Phillips began her life in basketball as a player at the University of Georgia. Unfortunately, an injury derailed her career on the court, but sparked her interest in a career as a coach and educator. She recently retired after 17 seasons as the head coach at Princeton High School, outside of Cincinnati, OH. She had a brief stint as Lakota East High School as well, leading their program for two seasons. In her time at Princeton, she was recognized as the Greater Miami Coach of the Year five times, the district coach of the year four times, and the OHSBKCA coach of the year in 2014. That same year, she led her team to only the second state championship in program history. Coach Phillips currently serves as a math instructor at Princeton.

I fundamentally believe that building relationships is the foundation of being a successful teacher and coach. It goes hand in hand with the quote, "People don't care how much you know, until they know how much you care."

My high school and college coaches were both very successful people who ran very successful programs; so winning was part of my background. They were similar in that they were both demanding and expected the best from their players. However, my experiences with each were very different and impacted me in different ways. Both were sources of motivation, as I joined the coaching profession, but in contrasting ways.

I endured mistreatment at the hands of my high school coach. That experience was difficult but formational, as it convinced me that it didn't have to be that way. I was going to prove that I could be successful as a coach, while treating players with respect and without playing mind games. My high school coach showed me what I didn't want to become.

My relationship with my college coach was much different. It had a very positive effect on my life, and I carried a number of important lessons away from our time together. I wanted to have that type of impact on my players! When I became a head high school coach, my goal was to win a state championship. But my mindset was that if I had to be like my high school coach in order to achieve it, I would NEVER win one, and I was okay with that. Fortunately, in 2014, we accomplished that goal and won a state title. I did it the right way. The night it happened, I got a congratulatory call from my college coach.

I think players have to know that you care about them as people, on and off the court. That is where the process starts. I care that my players are good students and I follow up with their grades constantly. I care that my players are respectful young adults, and if they are getting in trouble in school, I follow up. I care that my players are happy, have food to eat, rides to practice, rides home, etc. These things are the basis of building trust and respect, which lead to positive relationships. If you want players to run through a wall for you on the court, then, they have to know that you would run through the same wall for them.

At the high school level, I think it is very hard to be a successful coach and not be in the building. If a coach is showing up for only two hours a day for practice, how do you build relationships in this window? I have always taught in the building, where I have coached. Players know they can come to me at any time during the day, if they need something. They also know I can find them anytime during the day, if I need anything.

As a coach, the wins and losses come and go but the relationships last forever. Sometimes, you don't know the impact you are making until much later, but there is no doubt that these opportunities are the most rewarding part of teaching and coaching.

❑ Pat Fitzgerald—Head Football Coach, Northwestern University

A 1997 graduate of Northwestern, Pat Fitzgerald has led his alma mater's football program to unparalleled heights, both as a player and a coach. Pat was a two-time All-American at Northwestern, as well as a two-time winner of both the Nagurski and Bednarik awards. He led NU to Big 10 titles in 1996 and 1997, with a historic appearance in the '97 Rose Bowl. He was named head coach on June 7, 2006. In the subsequent 13 seasons, Fitzgerald has led the Wildcats to nine bowl games and was the 2018 Big 10 Coach of the Year. Pat also heads the AFCA ethics committee and is one of the most respected coaches in college football.

When dealing with young people today it is critical to have open and honest dialogue. You have to take the time to talk with them, and more importantly, to listen to them. Being a great listener allows you to better understand what motivates your players. This will then help you to ask the right questions and get the young person to open up with you.

The goal is to always be honest with young people and not tell them what they "want to hear," but instead, what they "need to hear." Advise your players like you would advise your own children. Once open, transparent dialogue is developed, real trust can begin to form. When trust is established, a healthy and real relationship can begin.

❑ Jerry Smith—Head Football Coach, St. Francis HS (NY)

Jerry Smith has been at St. Francis, just south of Buffalo, NY, for 38 years. He has been the head coach for 31 of those seasons. In that time, he has led the Red Raiders to the league title on 12 separate occasions. He has been named the Buffalo Bills Coach of the Week five times and the WNY Coach of the Year four times. Coach Smith served as the head wrestling coach for over a decade, as well, and was honored as the WNY Coach of the Year in that sport two times. He has developed and influenced alumni who have achieved at a high level in sport—10 of his former players now work either in the NFL or at the highest levels of college football.

In any consistently successful organization, relationships must matter. The people within the organization need to believe that those in leadership positions have their

---

best interests in mind. This particularly applies to a high school football program. It is essential that the players trust the coaches, and the coaches can trust the players.

At the high school level, I believe that it is important the players know the coaching staff will treat them fairly. However, there is a misconception that fairly means equally; it does not. Every person and situation is different, and one judgment does not fit all. The players must know that they are going to be heard. They must also know their situation will be addressed within the context of each individual, and using the standards of the program as criteria. The circumstances of the situation, the history of the student-athlete, their performance, and "buy-in" all factor in. Dealing with every player in the program with a "cookie-cutter" approach does him a disservice. We need to be fair, but we also need to treat them as individuals.

Another way to value the relationships is to be honest. Players and parents want the truth. In my program, any player who is not getting playing time will know exactly why that is the case. If they have any questions, we welcome the chance to talk about it. We will go over all aspects of what they need to improve on or eliminate. The conversations are straightforward and honest. We also believe the parents need clear-cut procedures on communication with the staff. Sometimes, the parents do not understand what type of situation the player should handle on their own or when a parent should call. I advise parents to ask their sons what they want to know, before they reach out to a coach. If the answer is not satisfactory, then feel free to call me. I am always willing to sit down with parents and the player to make sure everyone is on the same page. I rarely have those meetings.

If relationships matter in the culture of a program, you can see it when the team plays. You cannot hide a team that cares about and loves each other. You can see it in defeat, but more importantly, you see it in victory. It is a special thing, when you see them celebrating together, genuinely happy for one another. Without that, we are just of bunch of kids running around playing a game. Football is much more than that.

❑ Sean Sweeney—Assistant Coach, Dallas Mavericks

Sean Sweeney is in his 10th year as an assistant in the NBA, and is widely considered one of the rising stars in the league. He broke into the professional basketball with the Brooklyn Nets in 2013-2014. He went from Brooklyn to the Milwaukee Bucks, where he worked closely with Giannis Antetokounmpo. After four seasons with the Bucks, Coach Sweeney joined the Detroit Pistons in 2018 and spent three years there. In 2021, he joined Jason Kidd's staff with the Dallas Mavericks where he works with stars Kyree Irving and Luka Doncic. He also worked on staffs at the University of Northern Iowa and the University of Evansville.

Building relationships with players is a critical part of the coaching profession. In the NBA, one of the jobs of a coach is to be a leader by setting the example and holding people accountable to the standards of the team. In order to do this, it is critical to have great working relationships.

In today's world, we see more and more information that influences, promotes, and reinforces self-aggrandizing behavior. Coaches must be able to sift through all that. To help the players on the court, coaches must find ways to reach players with the information that matters, and present it in way they can process quickly and carryover to the floor.

As coaches, we are always trying to find ways to connect to all of our players. This is particularly important with young players, if we want to be able to reach them with the important messages. Young players, in their formative professional years, must develop and build good habits, if they hope to see success throughout their careers. In order to help them do that, we have to work at finding ways to relate to them. This does not mean to be friends with the players we coach, but more accurately, to be connected and trusted.

Trust is something that is earned. To earn trust, it is very important to be able to communicate with anyone with whom we work, but especially the players whom we coach. This means both talking and listening. By building relationships with players, we strengthen our ability to teach and the team's ability to succeed.

Professional basketball comes with a number of distractions, but at its core, how we teach and play the game still matters most. Without strong relationships, this becomes even more challenging. We must be willing to do the interpersonal work

Ivelin Radkov/Shutterstock.com

Trust is something that is earned.

with the players in order to give them accurate feedback that they will value—both in what they do well and what they need for their development. We must also be willing to listen to feedback from players. Some of the best coaching advice comes from veteran players. Those guys have immense experience that can be incredibly impactful in our attempt to be better coaches and teachers.

Basketball is a team game and requires everyone to be pulling in the same direction. "We are all in this together" is a common refrain. In order to truly "be in this together," we must have a connection that fosters both improvement and achievement. The relationships serve as that connection. It is more important than ever to build strong relationships in professional basketball.

❑ John Rittman—Head Softball Coach, Clemson University

In 2020, John Rittman came to Clemson and started their softball program after 30 years of coaching at the major college level. For 18 seasons, he led the Stanford Cardinal program to winning seasons every year, 16 straight NCAA-tournament appearances, 13 40-win seasons, and 16 All-Americans. His program also produced a national player of the year, earned five Super Regional bids, and appeared in two College World Series. Prior to that, John served as an assistant coach at Kansas, Washington, Minnesota, and Oregon. Coach Rittman is also a staple of the USA Softball staff, serving over ten years in the program. He has been on gold medal winning staffs at Olympic Games, Pan-Am Games, and World Championships.

I have been coaching the sport of softball for 33 years. Over those years, I have grown a lot as a coach and teacher. Early on, I based my success purely on wins and losses and making sure the players I coached earned their degrees. That's what I sold in the recruiting process and how I set my goals each year. In those early years, I certainly built a lot of great relationships, but it wasn't a focus or a goal. I definitely did not base my success on whether I had great relationships with the players I coached. I cared about every one of the players I coached and what was going on in their lives, but it just wasn't a priority.

Eventually, I figured out that building those positive relationships was truly the reason I got into coaching after my playing days. It was certainly not for the money—I started as a volunteer and didn't get paid a 12-month salary with benefits until my fifth year in the profession. I coached because of the opportunity to build those relationships with both players and staff. The comradery of being a part of something greater than yourself and the ability to work together toward a common goal is what motivated me. I once heard the saying, "players don't care about how much you know until they know how much you care." I made that a goal of mine and have coached with that in mind ever since.

Another one of my priorities I have set as a coach is to keep up with the changes that happen over time. I have taken a lot of pride in being a lifelong learner. During my career, society and the players have changed in many different ways. I have had to keep up with ever-changing technology. When I started coaching, there were no cell phones or computers. I've also had to change how I communicate with players. I have kept up to date with all of the different social media platforms to help in day-to-day communication and in recruiting. I have approached all of this change with a positive growth mindset. I realized I did not want to be a labeled as an "old-school" coach.

I feel like I have been able to sustain a certain consistency of success by making relationship building a priority. I have had many failures as a coach over the years, but I have not let those failures define me as a person. I have used failure and adversity to help me grow, and that is probably one of the things I want this generation of student-athletes to learn. Life is not always going to be easy; there will be adversity and failures along the way. Don't let your failures define you and realize that the process of dealing with adversity is just part of the journey.

ABOUT THE AUTHOR

Brian Polian has been a veteran coach in college football, having worked at the Division I level for over 25 years. His stops as an assistant include Michigan State, Buffalo, Baylor, UCF, Stanford, Texas A&M, Notre Dame, and LSU. He also served as the head coach at the University of Nevada, Reno, where he led the Wolf Pack to two bowl games in four seasons and unprecedented academic success. He was considered one of the top special teams coordinators in college football, with his units appearing at or near the top of the national rankings multiple times throughout his career. ESPN.com, Rivals, and 247 have also recognized him as one of the top recruiters in the country at the conclusion of various recruiting cycles. He has served on the AFCA Ethics Committee, as well as on the inaugural College Football Officials Competition Committee. In 2023, he shifted his focus from coaching to athletic administration as he was named Senior Director of Athletics at his alma mater, John Carroll University. Along with his undergraduate degree from John Carroll, he has a graduate degree from Baylor University. Brian and his wife, Laura, have two children, Aidan and Charlotte, and the Polian family resides in Solon, Ohio.

Courtesy of Joe Ginley and JCU Athletics